HUNKER

Brief Essays on Human Connection

Also by Michael Perry

Books

Population 485: Meeting Your Neighbors One Siren at a Time

The Jesus Cow

The Scavengers

Montaigne in Barn Boots: An Amateur Ambles Through Philosophy

Visiting Tom: A Man, a Highway, and the Road to Roughneck Grace

Coop: A Year of Poultry, Pigs, and Parenting

Truck: A Love Story

Off Main Street: Barnstormers, Prophets & Gatemouth's Gator

Roughneck Grace: Farmer Yoga, Creeping Codgerism, Apple Golf, and other Brief Essays from On and Off the Back Forty

From the Top: Brief Transmissions from Tent Show Radio

Danger, Man Working: Writing from the Heart, the Gut, and the Poison Ivy Patch

Big Boy's Big Rig: The Leftovers

Million Billion: Brief Essays on Snow Days, Spitwads, Bad Sandwiches, Dad Socks, Hairballs, Headbanging Bird Love, and Hope

Peaceful Persistence: Essays On...

Audio

Never Stand Behind a Sneezing Cow

I Got It from the Cows

The Clodhopper Monologues

Music

Headwinded

Tiny Pilot

Bootlegged at the Big Top

Long Road to You

For more information visit SneezingCow.com.

Hunker

Brief Essays on Human Connection

Michael Perry

The essays in *Hunker* originally appeared as "Roughneck Grace" columns in the *Wisconsin State Journal* and are reprinted here with permission. Some were also featured as monologues on *Tent Show Radio* (TentShowRadio.org).

Thank You

The *Wisconsin State Journal* crew, week after week.

Ben Shaw, doing it all.

Patricia Duyfhuizen, for a keen eye, keen knowledge, and a poetic touch. Also [comma] thank you for the commas.

My wife and daughters.

Mom and Dad, because so much is rooted in them and built on them.

Ever and always, the readers.

Contents

INTRODUCTION

EVERY WEEK FOR A WHILE NOW and until they don't, I write up a "Roughneck Grace" column for the *Wisconsin State Journal* and they print it. This book collects pieces published between March 22, 2020, and January 9, 2022.

Those dates pretty much coincide with the COVID-19 pandemic, and it is a presence in the pieces but less than you might expect or fear or hope. Each week I wobbled between feeling I was failing to meet the moment and feeling I was a grandiose fool to think anyone was asking.

But week after week, slowly at first, and then regularly, I received messages, emails, comments, and sometimes even a handwritten note from folks I felt I could trust: readers. In short, they weren't looking to me for advice or a "take" on the latest news blast or controversy or tragedy or variant. Instead they said they were grateful for a brief break from it all. Something to go with their morning coffee. Something to read before bed. Something that was anything but that other thing.

Something to lighten the hunker.

So many suffered over the time this collection represents. So many served humanity (and are serving even as I type this). So many showed up and did their job. Were *helpers*—and continue to be. Folks for whom a light essay did nothing. In the pieces that follow I hope you hear me say I understand and recognize this.

To hunker is not to cower. To hunker is to hang in there. To stubbornly persevere. To shore up your little circle. Bank your fires. Tend to the hearts beating beneath your own roof. Do what needs to be done.

Reader, it is my privilege to hunker with you.

Cow Barn Scent

As I WRITE THIS we continue to hunker, a natural and preferred state for me in lighter times, but suddenly a duty. That is all I will say for now, as any reference to current events will be outdated even as I type it. Instead, with respect and deference to whatever the state of things might have become, I'll settle into sharing something smelly.

While driving the four-lane just past sunset a few weeks back, I happened to look out the side window in time to spy a square of light at the base of a black hulk of barn. The open door was a memory portal, the long yellowy row of light bulbs above a walkway splitting two rows of cows standing tail-to-tail, just as they did in my father's barn. It is an uncommon sight these days, and gone far more uncommon after a deathly tough run of years for small farmers who still stanchion milk cows on either side of a white-limed walkway. I could almost hear the rhythmic *ch't-sshh, ch't-sshh* of the milkers hissing in rhythm, feel the warmth of the cows compressed beneath the hay stacked in the mow above.

And yet what came rushing back above all was the scent of the place.

If you didn't grow up on a small dairy farm, the idea of cow manure as a sweetly evocative aroma may be tough to comprehend. In fact it is a tenacious scent. I once wrote an essay entitled "Manure is Elemental" in which I described myself as "one of those well-scrubbed small-town boys who sat beside you at the basketball game and, upon removing a coat donned in a porch hung with chore clothes, released a layer of trapped air that rose warmly to your nose, and you thought, *farm kid.*" As I said at the time, the sweet note of dung did linger.

Whether squishing it through our toes as we stepped from pat to pat in summer pasture or troweling it into the gutter on a winter's evening when we were just happy to be working inside, cow manure was simply part of our environment. I like to say I grew up on the wooden end of a pitchfork, and there is truth to it. From calf to cow, their back-end production was nonstop. We were forever cleaning pens or running a spreader or scraping it off our boots on the hunk of steel I-beam Mom kept on the porch steps for the purpose.

No surprise then that the distant glowing barn door tripped my ol-factory recall above all. You town kids might wrinkle your noses; we barn boot bumpkins close our eyes, widen our nostrils, and enjoy. "Smells like money," the old-timers used to say, and while supporting that statement over the long term with a short barn has proven elusive, I'm grateful for however it is our memories and senses are interwoven so that even at 70 miles an hour with the windows up, I knew just how it smelled inside that barn. Fifteen miles later everything went to strip malls and parking lots. I countered by imagining the farm kid aroma wafting in my wake, following me right into town and past the city limits sign.

Right Now

We're all doing what we have to. I know you are too. I have always loved the word hunker, but I am not so sure now. We'll see.

We'll see. You hear that phrase a lot.

Apart from the standard instructions from reliable sources, it is not my place to tell you what to do. Everyone rides these things on the horse they drew. Everyone is working with different resources. I know with our two kids I've been straight but not dramatic. Calm in the room, maybe not always in my head. But as always and as ever I am grateful for my children, because they compel me to be the person I ought to be. I have often written of them as buoys and anchors and pintles (**pin**-tl: *a pin or bolt, especially one on which something turns, as the gudgeon of a hinge*) (great, now I gotta look up *gudgeon*) (**guhj**-*uh* n: *a small, European, freshwater fish, Gobio gobio, of the minnow family, having a threadlike barbel at each corner of the mouth, used as bait*).

Hmm. Guess I gotta read up on the history of the hinge. Maybe this afternoon. It's been a while since I read a dictionary. I got my grandma's 1942 Funk & Wagnall's over there; it's the size of a concrete block, and you'd be amazed at all the words they had even way back then before we added *awesomesauce* and *googling* to the list.

But: the children. They draw my focus in the very best way. Both in the big picture and the little moment. I was talking to my elder daughter today. She's home from college, only rather than the rushed weekend visit in which she passes through to grab a jar of pickles and say Hi to the old folks she's cooped back up with us for the foreseeable future. We were discussing how we've become so used to dealing with everything from one remove: via app, via tap, via virtual. And that part of what has so knocked society sideways is there is no downloadable fix. Which we knew, of course. We're not that far removed from reality. But it's still bracing when nature forces your hand. Especially in an age when even an oldster like me can download a virtual bubble level while standing in the chicken coop trying to get the nesting boxes straight. And that was two smartphones ago.

Speaking of nesting boxes and downloads, egg production has been holding up. Our younger daughter collects them daily, her chores serving as centering pintle during this time of disruption. The kid would be thrilled with this characterization, I'm sure. Perhaps I'll share it with her so she has something to chew over while working on the firewood pintle.

Everything is uncertain, always has been. I take nothing for granted, including my circumstance or yours. All across the asymmetrical front of this thing there are people putting their lives in service. If we're allowed it, the best air is outside our windows. It was a privilege to draw it in this morning, and I hope you have a chance at same, the clear scent of it a comfort until we can again throw ourselves open to the world.

MONOPOLY

The Monopoly game is set on pause, everyone's fake money and cardboard deeds stored in separate envelopes, and the tattered box placed atop the piano. Elder daughter has the upper hand in that she owns all the yellow properties and is loading them up with hotels. Genetics are a curious thing: Both her grandmothers are women of dignity and character who gleefully cut you dead at cards; you can feel their spirit every time she collects rent from those of us stuck with Baltic Avenue and a railroad.

There is a delicate balance between wishing everyone well and acknowledging the legions for whom this is not the case. Between staring down the beast and breaking eye contact now and then for the health of looking at something else. These little dispatches are definitely filed under the category of something else and are therefore submitted with deference to the vast ocean into which they drop. And every letter of every word is punched in place with the knowledge that additional legions of our fellow citizens are out there putting their future on the line. I want to declare my gratitude and continue to do my part beyond these pages.

Lately I've been digging into the back catalog of this column ("back catalog" being a high-end synonym for "oldies"), reading them into my phone, and posting them on YouTube. I go straight through, flubs and do-overs included. No fancy lighting, and my wardrobe is clearly off the back porch hook. In a recent episode, you could see the tracks of an excellent homemade bean soup down the front of my hoodie. And last night, because there were no others at hand and we share the same prescription, I read a piece about exploding tape measures while wearing my mother-in-law's fancy blue reading glasses. I won't be able to maintain the pace, and the trending views indicate the world has—as previously noted—something else to do, but I am intrigued by the number of folks who have emailed or commented that they love the flubs.

They're not hilarious flubs. They'd never make an "outtakes" reel. They're just garden variety stumbles. Mispronunciations. Inexplicable lip slips. Losing my place. Start-overs. All of which I am happy to provide. Start-overs, especially. Hoo, we could all use a dozen-eggs-worth of those right about now.

Last thing you need in these times is me over-analyzing myself talking into my own phone. In the midst of all that's happening, I'm just happy that the joy of human connection is predicated in part on imperfection and the willingness of others to not just see it in us, but accept it in us.

When we resume Monopoly, there is one glimmer of hope for we other three: Elder daughter put pretty much everything in hock to finance those plastic hotels. Nothing is certain. When my wife has cooled off about getting cut out of North Carolina Avenue, we'll pull the game down again, gather 'round the card table, roll the dice, and see how things work out. I own Park Place but not Boardwalk, which is like owning a Lamborghini when you can't afford the gas. Perhaps you know the feeling. Forward!

Peepers and Phone Calls

THIS WEEK WHEN WE FIRST HEARD the pond peepers, their natural cacophony was a chorus of reassurance. Even as nature threatens us, certain comforting cycles continue.

It is impossible to type out the preceding soft-focus observation without acknowledging those struggling beyond the sound of frog song. While the majority of us are working the wobble between fighting fear, preserving perspective, and keeping home and hearth together, others are plunged fully into a fight for life and the lives of others. There is no breezing past this.

I was on the phone with my neighbor Tom this morning. Closing in on 91 years, he is the walking personification of a tough old bird. He noted his wife Arlene will have been gone seven years this month. The idea of holing up alone is not something new for Tom. There exists an informal neighborhood association that checks in on him and keeps his driveway clear in winter, but in fact he resists much help beyond that.

We covered a lot of ground during our conversation. The nature and history of manure-handling technology; the concept of guardian angels; our shared fear of heights. Regarding the latter, mine was inborn; Tom's was precipitated a quarter century ago when a rung at the top of his ladder snapped and he fell 17 feet to concrete. One of the joys of Tom's storytelling is the inclusion of precision details; I guarantee if that ladder is still in a shed over there somewhere and if you put a tape to it the replacement rung will be within a six-inch range of the number quoted. My sister-in-law was a teenager on Tom's hay crew when the accident happened. Tom's voice conveyed the twinkle and crinkle of his expression as he recounted looking up from the concrete to see her staring down at him. "Eyes as big as saucers!" Even over the phone line I could see him rocking forward to slap his knee as he guffawed. It was good to hear him. I could put myself right in the dark kitchen of his house where we've visited so many times over the years. For now a phone call will have to do.

Yesterday our little family got out on the land and walked it. We heard the peepers as soon as we stepped outside, their volume swelling as we traversed the ridge, becoming deafening as we descended to the valley. Then we emerged at the edge of the pond, and they fell silent. Here and there ripples spread as an unseen singer dove for the mud. A pair of wood ducks squeaked away into the sky. I wandered off to look for antler sheds while my wife and elder daughter stood stock-still at the water's edge, trying to spot the suddenly invisible amphibians. Halfway up a deer trail I stopped and turned to look back to see the two of them, motionless and waiting, until the first frog croaked, and then another, joiners-in all along the bass and treble spectrum, until once again the world was crowded with song.

Late Snow

A WEEK AGO my neighbor Denny and I shot the breeze the way we do these days—me from the car window on the shoulder of the road, him standing well back across his yard—and debated whether or not to remove our snowplows. Having weathered well over a century of Wisconsin springs between us, we voted to postpone. This morning I called him from amidst the drifts, and we congratulated each other on our perspicacious procrastination.

To be snowed in during these times seems redundant, but so we were on Easter Sunday. We had eggs and ham and a warm fire, riches of the most basic sort and nowhere else to go anyway. We decorated some of the eggs, put a hit on the ham, then settled in for a jigsaw puzzle and cards. Also you can hide a lot of plastic eggs in just one little old farmhouse. We went plastic because there was a tub of them in the garage, and they don't smell funny if you leave them in the piano for a month.

This morning I started the plow truck and left it to warm up while I did the chicken chores. I stopped for a moment to breathe the clear snow-scrubbed air and take in the down-valley landscape, squint-brilliant in the sun. Then I turned my attention to the hens. They do not care to dip their toes in snow, and as we owe them for those eggs, I shoveled out a bare patch and scattered some corn.

Next I swung by the doghouse to let the cats out and noted the solar power inverter was at dead zero. So after I plowed the driveway, I waded out to the south-facing side of the granary, and sure enough, the winds had stacked a foot of snow atop the photovoltaic panels. I pulled out the roof rake with the plastic blade and began dragging the accumulation over the eaves.

The nature of the task had me looking skyward, and I was admiring the blue when it occurred to me that there wasn't a contrail to be seen. Our place is remote but lies beneath one of the main flight paths inbound to Minneapolis, and it's rare the sky is free of white lines or a silver glint. The same is true lately when I shut the chickens in at the end of the day. On clear nights the sky is filled with stars, but nary a one blinking and sliding sideways with seat backs forward and tray tables up. I once rafted the Grand Canyon with a river guide who was halfway through a trip when the Twin Towers went down. He remarked how strange it was to be in the canyon for a week and never see or hear aircraft. I had the same feeling, and it jerked me back into reality.

This gorgeous snowy morning is also reality. But the silent skies were a reminder of other reality. Or the reality of others. There is uncertainty in the silence. But the snow must go off, the show must go on. Across the yard in the farmhouse, the rest of the family is working, studying, doing what must be done. By the time I got to the last panel, melt-holes were showing in the first one. I stowed the roof rake and headed for the office, checking the inverter on the way. The snow-holes were allowing the generation of 75 watts.

Come lunchtime, I peeked again. The sun was spinning up a reassuring four figures. I went to the kitchen and converted some of the day's brightness into a grilled cheese sandwich. I hope you are well.

Coop Move

CHICKENS ARE ON THE UPSWING, one of the signs being yesterday our neighbor came and towed away our old coop. It's been sitting out back ever since we switched to a newer, bigger coop on wheels. I've been meaning to fix the old coop up and use it for housing chicks or maybe broody hens, but if you could see one end of the list of things I've been "meaning" to do, you couldn't see the other end. The new owner will at a minimum have to replace the rotted roof and patch woodchuck holes in the floor, but as they say in real estate, it has good bones, and he has a hammer.

It was good to see it roll out of here. It served us well for many years. It housed our very first flock of hens and many more after that, appeared on the cover of my book *Coop* when it came out in hardback (despite that, and despite its being surrounded by chickens in the photo, during the very first radio interview of book tour the host congratulated me on the release of my new book *Co-op*), and based on the fat-chalk princess graffiti still in evidence, served as a playhouse for our younger daughter.

In previous times I might have been maudlin about letting the coop go, because I am wired to be sentimental over everything from corsages to crowbars, but lately I find myself trending minimalist. Rather than pine for the past, I texted my buddy Mills, who helped me build the coop. Had I built it myself, it would be a pile of mismatched boards, having either A) never been actually completed (down in my barn there is a single stud wall representing a tree house I began building for my elder daughter when she was in grade school; she is now collegiate) or B) having already fallen apart (pretty much everything I've ever built has a self-destruction shelf date predicated on an over-confidence in drywall screws).

So rather than retain it, I texted Mills and let him know the coop was finding a second life, and then I scrolled through a photo album from back when we built it together with help from my elder daughter. All three of us are smiling at the camera with a happy goofiness that easily outlived the tar-paper roof now lying in wind-ripped strips behind the granary even as my heart warms to the image of my collegian daughter as a knob-by-kneed stripling two-handing a hammer. How often I fail to notice what joy comes from doing things as opposed to achieving things.

The neighbors who adopted the coop are relatively new to the block. They're a young couple with young children. The husband and I have been shooting the breeze now and then, doing the lean-and-spit dance of getting to know each other without prying. More than once he and his wife have included us in their rounds when they drop off homemade food up and down our county road. Whether it winds up kindling or cackle-castle, I'm glad they've got that coop. The world could use a few more good eggs.

Sharpening the Saw

THE SUN FELT GOOD ON MY NECK as I stood at the back of the truck sharpening the chainsaw. It was the year's first day of warmth without any subtext of cool. Just plain balmy. As I ran the file back and forth, tiny grains of metal filings accumulated on my fingertips and sparkled in the light.

The tabs that hinge the tailgate finally rusted through, so I've removed it until I can pick up replacement parts from the salvage yard. The hinge components bolt in place, and replacement is fairly straightforward as long as I can break the studs loose from the rust. A squirt or two of Liquid Wrench oughta do the trick. Or WD-40, if only for the scent of it. A simple fix, and it will be nice to have a tailgate that swings freely again. Your modern tailgate presents with more folding and unfolding options than an origami convention. In fact some of the advances appear to be terrifically handy, but ours is a 1994 model, and after a year of lifting and wiggling it into position in order to get it to latch, I'll happily settle for a simple swing and slam.

Also, because the bumper protrudes, I have to lean in slightly rather than get right over the saw as I work on it. The tailgate, on the other hand, provides a nice accessible workbench. Puts the saw right in your natural wheelhouse. And provides a place to put your beer. In my case, a sparkling water, and maybe that costs me some knucklehead cred, although the pamplemousse was lightly tinctured with essence of residual 2-cycle oil.

And so I scrubbed away at the chain, enjoying the solar power on my shoulder blades and the sound of fully-returned birds. We've been using some of our unanticipated home time to open up old farm trails and beat back the boxelder brigades, specifically those currently threatening to take over our septic system mound. It's been good—and frankly a privilege in these stay-at-home times—to get out there to lug and sweat and hack away. As a bonus we've got a head start on firewood. When we first moved to the farm, I impugned boxelder as fuel, but in fact when properly dried, it holds a sustained and lovely coal. I'm also told it makes a unique syrup, although we've never tapped any. Should I go that way, despite all the trees I'm felling, I've got a thousand more to choose from, and a thousand more springing up. Boxelder are the rabbits of the arboreal world.

After two circuits with the file, the chain was finger-prick sharp and ready to go. I topped off the fuel, then the bar oil, stored in a black plastic jug that had been absorbing the heat of the sun. In winter bar oil rolls out like caramel, stacking up on itself before settling in the tank. Today it poured smoothly, and shortly I was crossing the yard with saw in hand. Over on the south side of the granary the buds on the plum tree were tight as crochet knots. It was a blessing to walk and breathe in the open air.

Cut the Notch

An attempt to recover my youthful vigor by running a chainsaw for five days straight has met with mixed results. If I had anything to sweat out, mission accomplished. If I was looking to strengthen half my shoulder muscles while knitting the other half into intractable knots, I have similarly succeeded. If I had hoped to drop ten pounds, I would have had to stop eating like the lumberjack I'm not. But if I hoped to hit the hay at the end of the day and sink into the mattress with a happy groan and sleep like back in the farm kid days, well, yep.

Somewhere at the base of my brain is what I call "the mule chip," which is an imaginary microchip programmed to make the host work like the proverbial mule: slow, steady, and stubborn. The mule chip is an asset for those of us who rely on perseverance over panache. I will not beat you in a drag race, but I am always in your rear-view mirror, and if I disappear it's not because you left me in the dust, it's because I just tortoise'd right on past you.

That sounds braggy, so lemme re-reference that third word, "stubborn." Perhaps slow and steady wouldn't be so essential if I was less bone-headed. If I took a little more time to reexamine my abilities and chart a course less reliant on rowing against the river and more on sailing prevailing winds and currents. As I am well past the half-century mark, the odds on that one are growing slim. It's hard to teach an old mule new dog tricks.

This week's trick has to do with felling a tree in the direction you want. You don't just hack it off and hope. And you don't just cut a notch in it like the picture books. You cut a notch like a right triangle, with the "b" leg represented by an inward cut on the horizontal. Next you cut the hypotenuse inward and downward from above until the wooden wedge pops out. Then you cut straight in from the opposite side, on a level or a bit above the "b" leg. If you've done everything right, the tree will tip while still attached by a band of wood—a hinge, essentially—that keeps it from twisting or toppling sideways.

My notching technique is—as you might expect—average. I can aim a tree, but I won't be driving tent stakes, as the pros like to put it. But it makes me a better feller in every sense, including safety.

Among the residual lessons I retain from my EMT days and my farming and logging friends is that you are most likely to get injured right about the time you're getting ready to quit. You're tired. You're pushing to finish. It's tempting to take a shortcut, to let the weight of the day or the tool take over, to reach for something rather than approach it from the proper angle. When I kneel beside the next trunk in an endless grove of boxelder and find myself tempted to just zip through, rather than set the notch, I recognize it as an early sign that it's time to refresh my focus. When it happens a second or third time, I know it's time to throttle down and live to saw another day. To hit reset on the mule chip before it switches from asset to liability. To eat more than I've earned but sleep right on budget.

Letters

TODAY I WROTE THREE LETTERS on paper with a pen. There is the temptation to wax nostalgic about old-school correspondence, to mourn its decline, and to swear a solemn oath that I will revive the practice, but my faith in such resolutions has waned over time. In short, not everything has to be a movement.

Two of the three letters were thank-you notes. As a matter of fact all three were thank-you notes, but the third was a combination condolence and thank you, about which more later.

The first thank you was to a reader who sent a gift. Time and simple logistics preclude my ever adequately reciprocating all the good will and good things sent my way over the years (and I am not even beginning to address my email In Box or social media messages, which long ago exceeded my ability to individually respond—although I still read every one), but it feels good to put my thanks in ink whenever time and circumstance allow, and so I did.

The second thank you was to a reader and longtime passing acquaintance who wrote me a well-timed and heartening letter. He also included a boxed set of the works of Nassim Nicholas Taleb based in part on Taleb's referencing my longtime favorite French philosopher Michel de Montaigne. As a result I am now chewing my way through *Fooled by Randomness*, which in the early going I have found engaging enough to keep me going, but intellectual enough that I have to revisit some passages two or three times in order to tease the thread of the thought from the fuzz in my head.

The third letter was written to a man I have never met. A man who lives in New York City and recently lost his spouse. This man is from a small town in the Midwest but found his way to the Big Apple through a love of art, theatre, and music. I don't remember how I first happened upon him, but I began to follow him online some years ago. Our correspondence has been limited to Twitter exchanges and a smattering of emails. He is a freelancer, as am I, and his work—and even more so the matter-of-fact manner in which he approaches it—has long been an encouragement to me, albeit from afar.

It is one of those odd modern relationships in which I have observed this person in his work, observed him survive a near-death illness, observed him meet and marry the love of his life, observed him support her through a long-term illness, then just recently observe him losing her at the precipice of hope—and yet these observations have occurred via electrons across a 1,100-mile gulf. At this same distance I have watched him hit deadline after deadline, and often, when he conveys his joy over a painting or a production, I hear echoes of my farm-boy self, never quite sure I belong in the lobby of a theatre—much less backstage—or at the keyboard, and yet thrilled to have landed there and working like mad to see that I am allowed to stay.

And so it seemed I owed this man more than a click and a "like." I scratched out a note (my penmanship has always been schizophrenic; in these late digital years its shifting styles are exacerbated by a flat-out lack of practice) of sorrow and thanks, sealed and stamped it, then carried it to the end of the driveway with the other two, placed them in the mailbox, shut the door, raised the flag, and—content though I am on our back forty—envied them their journey into the company of good people.

Garden in the Rain

It is important we bless our children with sentimental moments, so today we herded them outside for an hour of transplanting tomatoes in the rain. So it goes when Disneyland is closed.

I am no farmer and therefore do not ride the roller coaster of meteorology with the same white knuckles of those whose livelihood falls and rises with the rain gauge, but we have just enough in the way of small-time crops that I maintain a low-level awareness of the earth's moisture content specific to our little patch, and as of late the soil has run crumbly and the fire bans have been on.

Yesterday we tilled and hilled but ran out of daylight before we got the seeds and plants in ground. Many of those hills are laid out in long rows and covered with sheeting, meaning when the rains came last night the soil beneath the sheeting was essentially wearing a raincoat. With warm temperatures and sun incoming midweek, we figured the best thing to do was plant in the rain, as the holes we poke in the sheeting to admit the plants will also admit the moisture. (If this is confusing or comes off as poor reasoning and poorer gardening, understand I am condensing the narrative, and my wife would like a word.)

As we stood in the kitchen and announced the plan, the youngsters swiveled their heads to the window and eyed the slanting gray rain with something short of joy, but when we parents pitched hot showers, a roaring fire and a free-choice evening as payoff, spirits surrendered. (In the first draft I typed "spirits brightened," but I try to get my facts right.)

It was a 12-15 mile per hour wind putting the slant in that rain, and I gotta tell ya right around the five-minute mark even Dad was ready to spin on one muddy heel and head for the house, but at the ten-minute mark we crossed the absurdity point of no return, and for the next hour, the wetter and muddier and more miserable we grew, the easier it went. We knelt in the mud like it was carpet, we let the wet trickle down our necks. We got all the tomato plants tucked in, transplanted a brace of shallots, planted beans, and seeded a bunch of vine crops. Between the rows slop abounded, but the plants looked better out of their pots and collared in the earth, and it was good to imagine the water seeping to the seeds and somewhere down there in the darkness a germ cell popping one eye open.

We bedraggled back across the yard and to the house, shedding the worst of our outerwear on the steps and the porch. As I kindled the fire I could hear the first of the hot showers beginning. There was a chicken roasting in the oven. Outside, the half-size maple leaves were sweeping a wet wind. The tomato plants were bending but staying put. They looked like children knee-deep and hugging themselves in a cold pool. The sun will feel good when it comes.

Voltaire Is Dead

This morning i rose at 5 a.m. and read the final chapter of Jean Orieux's *Voltaire*. This marks the end of a year-long tussle with the book, which is a 550-page pumpernickel loaf. I read it in fits and starts over the course of mornings and nights and sometimes lunch, marking it up as I proceeded. Knowledge retention has never been my forté (in high school and college I aced tests by cramming data that dispersed the moment I put down my pencil; consider me the intellectual equivalent of a dandelion), so I hope to give it a re-read one day and see if I still agree with myself.

It is helpful (albeit unnerving) to read all history against the present, and Voltaire provides lenses aplenty. The chapter I read this morning led off with the following quotation of the man: "There are two monsters that desolate the earth in peacetime: one is calumny, and the other intolerance; I shall fight them till my dying day."

"Calumny" is one of those words my dandelion brain retains just well enough that I think I know what it means but still look it up pretty much every time I cross it, and having done so again this morning I can tell you various dictionaries have it as the act of issuing false, malicious or defamatory statements about someone in order to damage their reputation. You get the feeling Voltaire would have been occupied with Twitter full-time.

In fact, that's a facile take (a dandelion brain specialty). As I—and others before me—have noted previously, Voltaire's predecessor Montaigne would have made a great blogger. Plato was the original content aggregator. These observations are cute but of limited use. At the moment I am focused on message over medium (a piquant perception in light of my typing this up as a newspaper column smack in our streaming age), and in Voltaire's time the Enlightenment was regularly swamped and swarmed by the dissemination of ideas through books and pamphlets, some corrupted by literary piracy, others curtailed by censorship, many driven by sensationalism, subversion, and insidious lies. It was the reader's responsibility to judge the messenger as much as the message.

Through it all, Voltaire danced and defended his own truth. For the details, you'd be better off with Orieux than me. I enjoy reading about the man because he was susceptible to all human pettiness, spent a lot of time on financial investments as a form of insulation against politics and religion (and equal investments of strategic flattery), but also rose again and again to defend the highest ideals, often on behalf of those least likely to be allowed them.

Five hundred plus pages of Voltaire, and here is my takeaway: Few currents flow smoothly or directly, least of all human behavior, and for most of us row-boaters, navigation is the key. "What our eyes and mathematics prove to us must be considered true," wrote Voltaire in the book's final quote. "As for all the rest, the only thing to say is 'I don't know.'" Those last three words compose one of my top five favorite phrases, from Voltaire to Montaigne to Plato and the Socratic paradox. When I closed the book the sun was up and so were the birds. How lovely is a common peaceful day. If I am to look you straight in the eyes, I must admit I googled "Socratic paradox" on my phone.

Not Monochromatic

It is the lamest disclaimer but sadly more relevant than ever: I hack these things out roughly a week before they go to print and public. Today, I feel the keystrokes go stale even as I strike them. What can I say that will be relevant, will be of any use, that will not insult your intelligence by the time you read it? That will sway anyone not already set?

Two days ago one of my cousins—not one given to social media—posted the Dante Alighieri quote "The hottest places in hell are reserved for those who, in times of great moral crisis, maintain their neutrality." You wouldn't know it seeing him walking down the street or in his office chair at the computer or having me do the driving after a flight of craft beers for him and a Coke for me, but he is a seasoned veteran of war, and by "seasoned" I mean don't ask, and I can't imagine what he thinks when he sees some dough-ball wannabe cosplaying dress-up soldier. But I know when we talked after I read his Dante quote and called, he had just finished cradling his weeping daughter at bedtime. The little girl and I share a matrilineage but not skin tone, and she had been watching the news.

This is no time for an old white boy like me to dole out sociology lectures. Some time ago a writer and paramedic named Daniel José Older turned me on to the concept of amplification. That is to say, rather than trot out your take, hand the mic—literal or figurative—over to someone who needs—who has *earned*—that microphone but wasn't given access. Amplify: I've tried to do some of that of late, whether sharing the book *Thick* by Dr. Tressie McMillan Cottom or the 2017 *Sojourners* piece by

Courtney Ariel, "For Our White Friends Desiring to be Allies." Even here I am taking the easy way out.

That craft beer run was a lark. The ostensible purpose of the trip was to purchase wood stain to finish up some closet trim. We dutifully bought the stain and had all good intentions of returning home, but that brew pub was right there across the street and the hockey playoffs were on, and then we got to talking life and philosophy and our rough-and-tumble raisings, and at one point we sent my cousin's wife a picture of the beer flight and said we were doing our best to choose the perfect varnish.

Our extended family is not monochromatic. In fact the beer flight was a decent representation of our family photos, from dark to light. That statement in and of itself is problematic because even as I make it to claim credence I risk casting family members as props—or more shamefully, shields. But it is relevant for you to know how it feels—even after only the most superficial or secondhand exposure—to hear their concerns and experiences dismissed. Or disbelieved. Or minimized. I don't drink, and that's one reason my cousin asked me to be the designated driver after he sampled those beers. But it wasn't the only reason.

I am not good at politics. I am not good at debate. I am not good at the last word. My job here week after week is light reflections and dad jokes. But this week, in the name of Dante and my cousin and the little girl who carries my beloved grandmother's name, I choose to amplify and hope I'm up to take on what comes my way.

Michael Perry

POTATO BUGS

THE POTATO BUGS HAVE EMERGED from the earth and ascended to the green leaves and we are at war. The battles go slow-motion, a lot of shuffling and bending and picking and sprinkling diatomaceous earth from a repurposed shaker of seafood rub. We can no longer simply stroll the rows and revel in the burgeoning greenness of it all, no, we are ever eagle-eyed for any sign of a striped beetle, for the fluorescent orange egg clusters, the greasy little larvae intent on stealing our hash browns from the top down.

I grew up in commercial potato country (and, family legend has it, narrowly missed out on becoming a potato magnate heir). There was a lot of spraying, some of it by helicopter, which we kids thought was just terrific, because when you are growing up in Chippewa County just short of the Rusk County line without a television, watching a man in a glass bubble swooping back and forth in his chopper is pretty much all the IMAX you're gonna get. When it was time for harvest, they knocked the plants out with a final spritz and then the potato picking machines arrived, and if you've ever run a potato fork I can say you flat drool over the idea of a potato picker you can drive. Sadly, Dad couldn't be convinced.

To this point we've kept the hordes at bay with our daily sprinkling, picking, and scraping, but I know from experience they haven't even gotten started. We've been doing some reading and are going to try mixing the diatomaceous earth into a sprayable dilution. We're also reviewing our stores of neem and spinosad. Some guides say to drop the adult insects into soapy water, but I smash them on the spot with a twist of my heel.

It is odd to despise an insect so, especially since each is just doing what it is programmed to do.

There is an irony here in that you can tell from forty paces that I don't really need any more potatoes. But a potato is not just a potato. We grow red ones and brown ones and yellow ones and fat ones and skinny ones, and who can imagine stew without them? Or to be cheated of the steam that escapes when you slit the skin and scrunch the baker to receive the sour cream or butter pat? Or the sizzle of them sliced thin and frying simply in the pan? What sad island is the roast without its potatoes tucked in all around?

So we'll put the back of our necks in the sun and keep up the good fight. There are more of them than us, but here is my note of hope: Last year we fought the potato bug battle to what appeared to be a draw, at best. They devastated a third of our potato plants. Left the stems stripped and the leaves lacy. Even worse, the weeds got away from us and outgrew the potatoes. Come fall, we took out the forks and cardboard boxes, and then had to go for more boxes, and then even more, because despite it all the ground was studded with potatoes of every sort. Sometimes when things are bad you just stick with it because somewhere down in the dirt there is fruit.

BIRDFIGHT

WHEN THE ROBIN DOVE at the eastern phoebe and commandeered the T-post perch, it occurred to me the last thing I wanted to witness this week was more conflict. Almost as quickly I pegged this as egocentrically dramatic on my part, especially since I wasn't the phoebe. Furthermore, the moment the robin moved on, the phoebe returned, and for the next fifteen minutes I observed as it alternately perched and pitched itself into the breeze on erratic fly-catching sorties. Sometimes nature exists to remind us we overthink things.

Our garden is set on the brow of a south-facing hill overlooking a broad valley. This topography funnels up a regular wind. Most days there is enough to sweep the mosquitos clear, although it is not uncommon to work at the weeding with a pack of gnats trailing the leeward side of your skull like a murmurous knot of whinging electrons. The first year we lived here I contacted a friend in the alternative energy business and told him we wanted to put up a wind generator. You think you do, but you don't, he said. Turns out, while we did have above average annual wind speeds, ours was—as our friend put it—a "dirty wind."

Well, I took that personally. But he clarified: By the time it arrived at our ridge the wind was a gusty, swirly mess, having been forced upward and over the embanked treetops. What you want for a generator is sustained, straight-line winds. And then there is the wind generator downside of having to do maintenance on moving parts parked forty feet in the air. So we spent our money on photovoltaics, which for thirteen years have just sat there filtering the sun through sand and extracting heat for our teakettle.

Dirty it may be, but the wind tumbling up that hill provides a perfect surf for eagles, hawks, and kites. Yesterday six turkey vultures were circling at various altitudes. The turkey vultures often drop to tree level and swing low across the yard. The chickens run for cover, closing ranks beneath the coop. One day early in our tenure here I looked up from my writing desk to see a turkey vulture perched atop the corn crib, staring beady-eyed at the chicken run. I reached for a shotgun, then googled first and saved myself some trouble: They don't kill chickens, and they are protected by the Migratory Bird Treaty Act. Sometimes I get a little too Hoss for my own good.

This spring we hung a swing from the maple that was forearm slender when my wife and I were married beneath it. Today I sat in the swing and worked on some writing. The tree is thicker than me now although it is possible I will catch up. It had been a day of shortcomings and mixed results. Among my greatest blessings I count the ability to count my blessings. The wind was dirty, but the air was clean. The garden was burgeoning. The pole beans were climbing. And having outlasted the robin, the phoebe was picking off gnats.

PLINKO TIME

We live in a time of reckoning, although the very act of typing those words compels me to examine my definition of "we." For so many, the news is old news. It is bemusing to catch myself declaring I am "tired" of this or that inconvenience when that inconvenience can be measured in months. For how many of my neighbors is "inconvenience" measured over a lifetime? Or generations?

The first half of this year has refreshed my gratitude for the three other people who share a roof with me. Their very presence drives me to address responsibilities beyond egocentric musing while my coffee goes cold. Whether it is walking witness in the streets or buckling down and doing the paperwork necessary to navigate a new financial paradigm related to health insurance and the electric bill, they drive me to do better. In return I work hard and—I mention it a lot, but it's in the job description—make dad jokes. Reviews are mixed.

My family—the *presence* of my family—forces me off wishy-washy. In my bachelor days I could dip, dive, and hide. Not so now, especially when one of my children is an adult and the other a teen. I can't just lie in the weeds, I have to answer questions, engage in vetoes and ratifications, and—toughest of all—mediate between our cocoon and festering reality. For instance, we have regular family meetings to revisit policy and procedure as it relates to a certain dread virus. We read up, we discuss, and then we do the best we can.

I admit I have slipped into preacher mode on the topic a time or two. Specifically if I am going to deride experts, if I am moved to hoot at a headline, it seems incumbent upon me to first read all the way down into the fine print, down there where the experts tell us right up front this isn't easy, this isn't certain, further work is required and in process. If you want certainty, I say drop a big rock on your little toe. Perhaps one day we will all sneeze freely again, but for now I'm gonna go with uncertainty over ego. I wear a mask to the farm store because barring fresh developments it seems at the very least neighborly.

On a lighter front, the chronologic arrangement of my family compels me to remain conversant on everything from contemporary dating trends, Kool-Aid hair dye, and K-pop. If Dad does nothing but read Voltaire and try to bend the arc of time with a typewriter, he may miss the worldwide release of the latest Black Pink single, and the beans will not be weeded.

I've been doing this long enough to know when I'm not operating smoothly. When my thoughts are disjointed. When a column is less roller-coaster than bumper car. When the central theme tracks like a clown riding a pogo stick home after the tavern closes. Regarding this column specifically, I admit we have arrived at the penultimate paragraph in the manner of a Plinko disc on *The Price is Right*.

There is no ribbon sufficient to put a ribbon on this, so howsabout a pastoral reflection? I had the profound privilege of finishing this column at dusk on the brow of a hill as the sun went down. Literal peace. Right at the end, a pileated woodpecker dipped past, backlit and prehistoric in profile. Just as he dipped from sight and into the trees, he canted his head my way and, speaking very clearly, said, "You people are idiots."

I was still working on a comeback when the stars came out.

Hanif and the Birds

RAIN IS DRIPPING FROM THE LEAVES in the aftermath of a morning thunderstorm. The skies are still gray. There are no shadows. Last week someone asked who was my favorite poet. I am on speaking terms with just enough poets to know better than to name names. Furthermore, the act of ranking poesies is a silliness akin to stringing squash racquets with spun sugar; it leads to a pointless game and makes a mess of something sweet. More importantly, have you ever heard birds sing as the cloudburst fades?

I did go so far as to say you could do worse in this historic moment than reading the collected works of Lucille Clifton, who knocked me off my slice of comfy white bread over thirty years ago. There is much to be learned from the late Ms. Clifton's works regarding brevity, bravery, boldness, clarification, scarification and—when earned as such—celebration of the human as a whole.

I have just deleted the paragraph that followed the one above; it morphed into a recitation of the names of poets who have held the greatest sway over me over time. I am forever grateful for and will forever re-read their work, but the line between recitation and regurgitation, of reverence and somnolence, requires attention. Reminiscence is a righteous form of restoration until it obscures the vital present; rather than trot out my wellworns, let me cast my eyes down and to the right of my well-worn reading chair and tell you I see (and recommend) three titles by the poet, essayist, and cultural critic Hanif Abdurraqib: *They Can't Kill Us Until They Kill Us, The Crown Ain't Worth Much*, and *A Fortune for Your Disaster*. I once observed as Hanif read his poetry from the balcony of a tiny house tuned and wired for sound while it was played by musicians during an alternative music festival. Twenty-five years earlier, in that very same field, I whooped and hollered through my one and only Waylon Jennings concert. Both men were solidly on message and I love cultural caroms.

Yesterday after picking potato bugs beneath an exfoliating sun but no other weather, I had taken to the shade of a maple with a cool drink of water in hand when a gigantic oak not fifty yards away spontaneously split in two and sent one half of itself crashing to the forest floor. It took several smaller trees with it, and the noise was louder and went on for longer than you'd think it would, and naturally this rendered the subsequent silence capacious indeed. As non sequiturs go, this was a real organic crackerjack. But as with today's departing thunderstorm, birdsong flowed quickly back in.

I notice birds have been cropping up in my writing a lot lately. I'm no ornithologist and hardly a mystic, but as with poets I suspect it has something to do with their willingness to sing for us even when we don't deserve it.

Ennio Morricone

I SPENT THE BULK OF THE DAY listening to the music of Ennio Morricone. I'd like to cop a knowing pose regarding his oeuvre, but in fact I am not a film buff and went on this listening bender because I read on Twitter that he died. So it is our days are directed. Based on what I've heard so far today, Mr. Morricone was good at summoning sensations of sweeping poignancy. This has been no help at all in getting the chores done.

My susceptibility to sweeping poignancy is one reason it might be best I'm not employed in a rougher profession, although I know from a few heart-to-hearts with my brother the logger that the tougher trades are not impervious; he just doesn't spend a lot of time typing about it. That said, last time we chatted, the evaporating pulp market coupled with a strong American dollar versus the Canadian loonie and some related international trade issues had him trending lugubrious. Nonetheless, off he went and sharpened his saw.

Following on his example, and despite a passage from the "Father Ramirez" theme that plucked my heartstrings like a sad Spanish guitar or the stretches of "Love Theme" that had me resisting the urge to grab my notebook and run upstairs to write pie-eyed free verse in my room like it was eighth grade crushes all over again, I curtailed my poignant swoon-time and got back to business with the mundane realities of balancing the checkbook, getting the camp chairs off the lawn before it rained, doing some rototilling, and watering the chickens.

Speaking of which, I am hardly your leading environmentalist but would like some bonus recycling credits for watering the chickens with the five gallons I collect from the twin dehumidifiers in our basement every morning. There is the added health benefit of climbing the stairs while carrying forty pounds of water. This morning I had a little extra left over, so I tipped it out along the row of sweet corn I revealed last night, which is to say I finally pulled the weeds that were taller than the corn. Had to do it by hand as you cannot rototill weeds that tall unless you are really into round bales packed with clay. Knee high by the Fourth of July, the old-timers used to say, problem being, they weren't referring to the pigweed.

Eventually I made it back to the little room over the garage and played some more Morricone. He did run the gamut. It doesn't all sound like a Clint Eastwood Western. It isn't all pensive. The cellist Yo-Yo Ma said Morricone thought of music as "energy, space, and time." That's about right on. Each track filled my mind and heart with pictures, and how fortunate I felt to peck away at my deskbound tasks in a safe space filled with evocative sound. At a press conference announcing Morricone's death, his attorney read a statement written by the composer himself: "I, Ennio Morricone, am dead." As final verses go, that's tight.

Wren Parents

The three fledgling wrens outside my window found their wings and fluttered into the future last week. After a few days of empty-nest silence, the male is now back to singing all day long and hosting showings for prospective partners. Yesterday, after coaxing an interested party in for a look, he dropped to an eave of the bird house and pointed toward the entry with his beak while cupping and drumming his wings as if to usher his visitor forward. She went as far as poking her head through the opening a time or two but departed without entering. As of this morning he's still out there warbling, the sonic equivalent of a sign-spinner perched outside a new development doing his best to divert commuters to peek at a spec home.

Meanwhile last week's weather reminded my wife and me of our formative years spent stacking hay bales no matter how hot and humid it was and how we accomplished this—brace yourselves—despite the utter nonexistence of smartphones or Bluetooth earbuds.

As with many parents of our age and background, we are young enough to be hooked on all the same digital doo-dads as our kids and yet old enough to remember life without them. It's an interesting spot in which to be caught, having to pause your podcast or drag your eyes off of Twitter long enough to lecture Tomorrow's Hope on the importance of meatspace chores and boredom in the development of character and a well-rounded mind.

One also faces the futility of constantly comparing and contrasting our own past with our children's present. Even as I launch into a By God disquisition on why it is we must learn to stack wood without a K-pop soundtrack, I am echoing (if not word-for-word, then harrumph-by-harrumph) my own father's inveighing against my not picking up my pitchfork until I found a place to prop my pre-boom box cassette player (with the red "record" button) beside the heifer pens so that I might toil to the tune of one of two albums approved by my younger brother: "The Sensational Charley Pride," or a collection of country covers by former NFL quarterback Terry Bradshaw. My brother was a bit of a straight-shooter and thus vetoed Queen's "A Night at the Opera." For the record, we enjoyed that Terry Bradshaw album, although one might question whether we'd have noticed should the tape have gone garbled.

The thing is, with those cassettes, you pushed play and that was it for 20 minutes or more. You could get some manure moved. Whereas based on my field observations, what really slows the workflow with digital music is the non-stop curating. So much tappety-swipe. Then again, I derail my own train of thought to observe that "non-stop curating" is the perfect description of parenting. So often it feels that child-rearing is accomplished in thirty-second increments of "*what now?!?*"

You preach a little, you adjudicate as best you can, you love a lot, you smile and listen to the music that moves them whether you're feeling it or not, you make them listen to a little of yours now and then, and after it all they tip from the nest and flutter away. By the time they skyline the horizon you're praying they'll survive to migrate back now and again. You need to fill the silence without evocation so you cue up some bland anodyne on the order of a "Peaceful Piano" playlist. Soon enough you shut that down so you might simply listen to the wren sing.

Self-help Rooster

Our rooster managed to escape the fence and now can't figure out how to get back in. I don't feel sorry for him because he is an unlikeable fellow given to preening, false bravado, and egotistical uselessness who eats feed but doesn't lay eggs. We shoulda stuffed him in a stewpot long ago, but I keep him around as a feathered barometer to monitor my own character; when I note my demeanor beginning to overlap his, it's time to correct course. I have been known to lay both metaphorical and artistical eggs, and I regularly eat more feed than I've earned.

When I arrived to do the feeding and watering this morning, there he was, clucking and tut-tutting outside the run. "Don't know what to tell ya, bud," I said. "You made your choices." Talking out loud to chickens is standard operating procedure around here. They're not great listeners, but they are physically unable to roll their eyes, thus sparing me a most common reaction when I get to babbling on the home front. I left the gate open to see if he'd reenter while I distributed the scratch grains, but he was so focused on running territorial laps and interrupting himself to crow that he failed to note the opening. So I closed it and let the hens out of the coop. As I walked away he was crowing through the fence at the chickens within, assuring them that, although out of bounds, he was still the boss.

In my office there is a book approximately the dimensions of a box of doughnuts. It is a motivational tome composed by one of those professionally inspirational multi-platform one-percent-body-fat 300 IQ overachievers (or at least his "team") who spout just enough bullet points to get you to buy the book but nowhere near enough bullet points to fill the book without a lotta rhetorical padding (I know the feeling).

Nonetheless its heft conveys commitment, especially the first day of the rest of your life when you sit down with it and resolve to finally get yourself in gear. This weekend I paged through it for the first time in over a year. I was moved to do so by a discussion I'd had with my cousin Steve—an actual achiever—about books that had been a help to him. I brushed the very literal dust off the cover, placed it atop my laptop to establish scale, snapped a photo of it with my phone, then texted the photo to Steve with the following caption: "I don't read it, just lift it three times, hit a protein shake, and ROLL."

This earned me a ROFL. I was about to follow up by snarking that of all the book's 675 pages, I had benefited from maybe three, when I randomly opened it, and there on the page was a section I'd incorporated into my daily routine since the day I read it. Dedicated to my disdain, I'd completely forgotten that one of those bullet points had actually struck home.

Don't get me wrong. That book is still mostly filler. The bullet point was a mild dietary thing. But I moved the book over beside my reading chair again. Tonight when I close up the coop I'll leave the gate open. Come morning I expect that rooster will have found his way in. "Newsflash, bud," I'll say. "Sometimes if we stop crowing long enough to revisit the source, we help ourselves in spite of ourselves."

The hens will ignore us.

Screen Door Spring

THE WOODEN SCREEN DOOR BANGS SHUT behind us now that I replaced the spring, and that right there is one of your Top Five civilized sounds. Not *too* civilized, or you'd have one of those slow-moving hydraulic jobs, but where's the fun in that? If you prefer a screen door that makes a squeezy sound then gently tamps itself into the doorframe, so be it. I prefer something more definitive.

There is some irony in this as just this morning I griped that we live in a time desperately short on nuance and grace, which you could say a hydraulic screen door represents. Still, I prefer the slappy slam. It echoes nicely off the granary and off my memory. Because that's it, isn't it? A slamming screen door is not so much a sound as an evocation. In fact my affection for the screen door slam is such that it overrides my latent hyperacusis, a fancy name for a condition that renders sharp noises painful (and the listener grumpy). The screen door gets a pass because it triggers so many palliative associations.

I used to write for a magazine called *No Depression*, which took its name partly from a song called "No Depression" recorded by the Carter family in 1936 and partly from an album called "No Depression" released in 1990 by a band called Uncle Tupelo, which contained a cover version of the song "No Depression" as well as an original tune called "Screen Door," which is where the music magazine *No Depression* got the idea to publish the closing essay of each issue under the title of "Screen Door."

You follow?

Doesn't matter. Point is screen doors speak to us of other times and other porches and open air and roomy afternoons and music from a distance and the freedom of coming and going and a form of sonic time travel in which every wood-slat slam is tied somehow to a memory just beyond our grasp. Which is why after half a summer of our screen door hovering helplessly between open and closed and letting the bugs in I finally took the cordless screwdriver in hand this afternoon and fixed it. "Fixed it," in scare quotes, because what I did is sink a cheap drywall screw into the door frame and hook the new spring over the Phillips head.

But man, it snaps smartly shut. I didn't tell my wife. I figured I'd let her discover it like the gift it is. Let her wonder about the identity of the anonymous handyman until she sees that drywall screw, at which point it will become self-evident.

She came home this afternoon and has been in and out of the door a couple of times. So far I have received neither notice nor acclaim. I am going to try real hard not to ask. She has been known to respond to my fishing by fixing me with a look normally reserved for needy kindergartners and asking if I would like a gold star. Just now it occurs to me that perhaps she was hoping for a hydraulic screen door that closes with a velvety *tunk*. This is the sort of critical mismatch premarital counseling often fails to address. I shall propose it as an agenda item for the next family meeting. Nuance and grace are in the ear of the beholder and sometimes you just have to create your own.

Virtual School

As i was typing the first draft of this column, an email pinged in from one of our local school districts. Attached was the pandemic attendance plan. It was carefully composed and thoughtfully presented. It will be met with joy, trepidation, and resistance. And may be moot at any minute.

Where would we be without people who give their best? Right now everyone involved in education—from parents to professors—is dealing with their own frantic calculus. Some have options; some have none. Even with school-age children of my own (one in middle school, one in college) and facing my own difficult decisions, I know that all around me parents, teachers, and support staff are facing challenges far more complex. There are so many variables and combinations. Single parents. Lack of daycare. Lack of food. Of funds. Nonexistent internet. Number of children in the house. No house. Politics. Disinformation. Or solid information that is nonetheless tough to navigate.

Through a mix of privilege, chance, challenges, geography, and other variables I am not sharp enough to identify or recall, my children have participated in a potluck's worth of educational settings. Over time they have attended standard public school, Montessori classes, public charter schools, virtual school, home school, and quality time with their elders. In each and every setting, the format was less important than the teacher. I say that first and foremost with public school teachers in mind, as— based on my firsthand observation—they deliver more than expected for less than they deserve. But I am also recognizing those parents out there suddenly thrust into the role of homeschooler and doubting themselves.

I read a quote today that said, "Science self-corrects." This is both an implication of error as inherent to the process and *progress* through the process. Whether we convene classes on the family couch or in the public classroom, we are going to take wrong turns, we are going to have to reverse course, we are going to have to regroup and reassess. The idea that we can simply declare ourselves geniuses without checking the math has passed its expiration date, and we are paying the price.

A while back after making offhand public mention of our homeschooling experience, I received correspondence from a professional educator upset that I would reject public schools; conversely, another individual warmly congratulated me for rescuing my children from the grip of "lefty thugs." I know I'm not the only one weary of public dialogue as a version of poisonous ping-pong, with both parties going for the smash. I am not cut out for it and in fact would prefer sitting in a quiet room smacking myself in the head with the paddle (I trust some of you will second the motion and maybe even provide the paddle).

We are not all in this together; by now that has become obvious. But a *lot* of us are in this together. And for those of you doing the best you can in the circumstances you're stuck with, whether you are teaching in a socially distanced classroom or over the internet or at the kitchen table, know that today's children will remember their teacher not so much for the lesson but for the commitment. They sense who has their best interest at heart. They'll grade us later. And many of you, despite all challenges and despite all doubt, are earning extra credit. Thank you.

FOMO

Yesterday i shared my failure with the world, and the world was delighted.

This spring we planted a few rows of sweet corn along the far outer edge of the garden. After a strong initial sprout, the corn was overtaken by weeds. I beat back the assault with some hoeing and pulling, but then the potato bug wars began, and the next time I checked in, the tallest of the corn had grown to four feet.

The weeds had grown to five.

Through a combination of whacking, scything, ripping, yanking, grunting and sweating, I cleared the entire patch. When it was done I stepped back, planted my fists on my hips, and surveyed what I had wrought. This ceremonial moment is the working class equivalent of the cleansing breath.

That night a storm blew in and knocked three-quarters of the corn flat. The wind was strong, but the damage was mostly due to the spindly and anemic state of the stalks, so long shadowed in weeds. By morning the tender bits of the toppled corn had been nibbled by the deer that had previously been kept from the plants by a phalanx of pigweed so stout you coulda cut 'em into 2x4s.

Fast forward and we are headed for a sweet corn harvest that will be measured not in ears but kernels. It's a sad little stand, mangled and sparse. Yesterday on a whim, I pulled out my phone and snapped a picture, then posted it to Instagram with the following caption: "This being the season of bragging on gardens, I herewith submit the antidote to FOMO: behold our sweet corn."

It turned out to be one of the most "engaging" posts I've put up in months. All kinds of folks weighed in with laughter emojis, good-hearted gibes, and humorous retorts of their own: "Stick to writing!" "Nice weed crop!" "It looks like your corn is social distancing." "You can make stir fry with those tiny corns!" "Snack size…reduced carbohydrate!" "Did that corn volunteer, or was it drafted?" "I'm allergic to corn, so this is perfect." One fellow told of his beautiful corn, which he gave "just one more day" to ripen…and of course that night raccoons stripped every single stalk.

But more to the point, there was the person who asked, "What's FOMO?" I explained Fear Of Missing Out as a form of envy based on other people's social media feeds implying their lives are perfection.

True confession: Before I photographed that corn, I snapped a shot of a bountiful box of our tomatoes, cucumbers, and onions, intending to post it. But that picture wouldn't have told the real story…about all the family and friends who have helped out this year, about how some of our garden is doing terrifically well, some of it medium, and other patches gone the way of our sweet corn.

I'm glad I went with the failure picture. We are surrounded by the facade of everyone but us having it together. Thus we find joyful unity in a flop. It was refreshing to see comments like, "Same here but even more scraggly!" "LOL this makes me feel so much better." "You must use the same no till method I do." There is a grander point to be made here about displays of vulnerability as code for shared struggle, but instead I leave you with the commenter who said, "Looks exactly like my husband's," and all the possibilities that invokes.

Camping

A FEW YEARS HAVE PASSED since I last tent camped, and the irony struck me at dawn: While I have never been more well-padded, I have never felt the earth more sharply. Put in terms of inverse proportion, apparently as I get softer the ground gets harder.

I am typing on deadline at a streamside picnic table in Montana. The tent is folded, the van packed, and Beartooth Pass awaits. When we departed on this trip, we stopped to check in with our neighbor Denny down the hill, and he said he got started on the Beartooth once but had to turn around and go back, which is to say, hills are relative. Denny's not a timid man, so I'm a little nervous about the itinerary. I claim no victory before its time, and we are furthermore driving a big honking van.

I don't want to turn this into the prose version of trapping you with our family vacation photos, so I'll keep the observations random. It is a distinct time to travel. The open road feels more freeing than ever, but at each refueling stop we put on our masks and feel a bond with anyone similarly attired, and slightly foolish in the face of the others. So it goes. We are traveling in a family pod of four and hiking outdoors so in the main, mask tensions are low.

Long hours behind the windshield are conducive to reviewing your worldview, and so far my most profound observation (I'm claiming it as profound, since no one else will) occurred while crossing North Dakota and considering gophers. All my life I've been entertained by the way they scoot across the road, their little legs spinning like a overwound toy as they sprint to avoid the onrushing traffic. Or at least that's how

I've always interpreted their mad dash. But somewhere out there on the prairie, when yet another striped rodent shot across the centerline, it occurred to me: Maybe that's how they *always* cross the road, even if there's not a vehicle in sight. Perhaps they scramble because they know the pavement leaves them utterly exposed to hawks. They're not avoiding death by radial, they're avoiding death from the air. The question at hand is a slight alteration on the popular "tree falls in the forest" thought experiment: If a gopher crosses the road and you're not there bearing down on him at 70 miles an hour, does he still run?

Before taking on the Beartooth, we stopped to visit a man who did our family a good turn once. Today he fed us breakfast, gave us elk sausage to go, and entertained us with an impression of Barney Fife attempting to wield bear spray. Understand, this man played offensive tackle in the National Football League for a dozen years. You really haven't lived until you've watched a 6'7" professional grade lineman dancing and fumbling in the persona of America's favorite skinny deputy.

I type this final paragraph fourteen hours later. We made the Beartooth and spent the day wending through Yellowstone National Park. It was a glorious day of mountains, vistas, and bison. Tonight I sleep on a mattress. It is soft, like me.

Michael Perry

Big Sky

We are back in the Badger State.

It was a seven-day run, with stops in North Dakota, Montana, and Wyoming. No offense, Minnesota, but we are neighbors and visit you plenty and this time just gave you a wave. Perhaps we'll drop in with the Packers should normal times return.

As family trips go, this one was transitional. Our daughters are now 20 and 13, and we scheduled the trip so the elder could ride along between summer classes and the fall semester away at college. She is on her way to living her own life and already goes on adventures without us. This is as it should be, and yet I still marvel that I no longer need buckle her into her safety seat or fish her juice box out from between the cushions.

The sisters miss each other terribly when they are apart, and for upwards of three minutes when they reunite, after which it's back to the usual eye-rolls and bickering. Our time in the van has been what you might expect, although to be fair they are not the only ones riding a sine wave roller coaster of sweet and sour. Things go in and out of phase. Mom and Dad included.

Outside of the van, we hiked a big hunk of Yellowstone National Park, our blisters and weariness at the close of the day only magnifying the size of the hunk of Yellowstone we'll never see. We walked downtown Bozeman, we explored the trails around Big Sky, and my wife and elder daughter were turned away from one adventure because "Tom Brady is building a house up there." I had this terrific vision of Tom on drywall stilts, but I'm pretty sure he was at football practice and not actually suited up in a tool belt and nailing down chipboard. The fact remains, you are not invited.

Wherever we went, COVID-19 permeated the atmosphere in the figurative sense as much as the literal. We maintained our masking and distance and attended exactly zero raves. At some point during the trip I began to focus less on the maskless and more on the maskers, as they gave me hope and everyone likes a helper. In this particular game of shirts and skins, I favor shirts.

My wife says I am afflicted with horse-to-the-barn syndrome, and she is not wrong, as we left Big Sky in an early morning haze of wildfire smoke (From which fire, you ask? Pick one.) and rolled into our yard at 3:30 a.m. to find I'd left the light on in the granary all week. I strolled out and shut it off then stood in the yard and stared at the stars. Our constellation-cover can't match the Montana backcountry, but there's still more of 'em than you can count, and they always do their job, which is to swallow whole every self-pitying thought I might have had of late. America's a big country even when you only cross a third of it, but it's not so much as a microscopic mote among those stars, which, if you stare at them long enough, draw you right out there to float in airless silence, a form of purity we all long for at one time or another.

Songwriter

A SONGWRITER UP IN CANADA sent me a note today asking to see a picture I'd posted on Instagram over three years ago. It turns out he had used a portion of the caption as a line in a song. This is the sort of fragmentary interconnectedness that gives me joy in the face of all the digitized heartlessness surrounding us.

I met the songwriter once in a Minneapolis coffee shop. He was playing in support of another musician of my acquaintance, and she felt we might hit it off. Indeed we did. Making a living via keyboard or fretboard is not "hard" by the physical standards set by my rural Wisconsin youth or your average underwater welder, but as with any boutique hustle—be it running your own repair shop or your own dance studio—chances to talk shop with someone who understands it's not all dreams and musing are few and far between. Even artists like to discuss per diems and standard business mileage rates.

Over time the songwriter and I have maintained an intermittent correspondence, often in the wee hours, when we message each other about working at our profession when our families are abed or home while we are on the road. I find it interesting that we don't call each other. It's almost as if we wouldn't know what to say on the phone, whereas we're well used to sending words blindly out into the world.

On some level our relationship is easier too in that we are both married with children and happy to be so. We are hooked on our work deeply enough to stick with it even when other vocations might float a better boat beneath us, and yet rather than wild riders at the gates of dawn blasting through society's norms, we are in the end dads with responsibilities. This too gives us something to talk about.

There is this intangible thing I am ever more grateful for daily: The sense that quiet, solid people are daily at their quiet, solid work. To drive our country road having just switched off the national news and see that the guy with the sawmill is making boards but—as it says on the spray-painted slab—is available by appointment only. That the woman who delivers our mail is making her rounds, delivering not only our correspondence but our business...and our ballots. That the county maintenance crew rose early and cleared the windstorm debris from the road.

I need not see these people in action to appreciate their presence. The songwriter, for instance: It is nice for me to type a message in a virtual bottle and drop it in the internet stream and know that in his tiny backyard studio up there in Canada he may or may not hear the ping, but he will respond in time, and whatever the distance, we are working beside each other in spirit. Not nosing in, not telling each other how to do our jobs, but now and then giving a nod. Sometimes we marvel at how the world could be.

The Apple Game

"Tío Mike, can we do the game where we run and throw apples?"

My godson—mi ajihado, as his father taught me—is seven years old, and I had no idea what he was talking about. He and his parents had come by for the now-normalized distanced outdoor visit. We hadn't seen each other for some time, and the apple-throwing reference wasn't ringing any bells.

"You know!" he persisted. "We run, and then we throw an apple."

And then it came back.

Since the day he took to his feet, this kid has been an athlete, zipping around at triple speed. In fact, even before he could walk I remember him sitting in his diaper and whipping wiffle ball strikes to his father, who grew up in the streets of Panama and had a cup of coffee—or at least an espresso—in the Baltimore Orioles farm system. My godson's two older brothers excel at baseball as well. Between the three of them, Tío Mike secretly harbors a hope that he will one day get to sneak on the field prior to a Major League game. I am also proud of their wit and engagement outside of athletics and do my best to tell them so.

My godson's inherent athleticism is matched by a desire to employ it at every turn, which is to say sometimes babysitting him means running laps. And that's where the apples came in.

When I am on a fitness binge, I have this circle workout I do in the yard: Start at the pole barn, sprint up a sharp, short hill, then walk back down to the pole barn and repeat. Last year around this time the godson was visiting and feeling rambunctious so I asked him to join me. "We'll do six laps," I said. Then I lined up six apples in a row. "Every time we finish a lap, you can try to throw an apple over the barnyard fence. When the last apple is gone, we're done."

Apparently this made a big impression, because here he was a year later asking to do it again. So we lined up our apples and went to it. After slinging the third apple he looked up at his chest-heaving sweat-ball of an uncle, and asked, "Do you do this every day?"

"Oh, no," I said between air gulps.

And then he reached out, patted me on the gut, and said, "Well, you should."

When that boy was baptized I stood right there in church and took a solemn oath to protect and care for him, and as his padrino I will keep my word, but now and then from the mouths of babes come frank assessments that test the bonds. We did another three laps, and I let him sling the final apple at the bald-faced hornet's nest along the pole barn eaves, and of course even throwing from up on the hill, he bounced it off the tin within a foot of the target, and as they came boiling out, he ran for the house on a beeline blur, leaving me all flat-footed and fading fast. The scene of him diving into the house just ahead of the screen door slam is frozen in my fuzzy head and will bring me a smile long past the time I am able to run and throw apples, a memory the boy unlocked therefore locked in.

Massage Music

Lately i have taken to working while listening to a playlist called Ambient Space Soundscapes, otherwise known as Welcome to Your Massage Appointment. The results have been mixed.

The whole thing began when I found myself in one of those funks where every genre of music I cued up—from Beethoven to heavy metal covers—evoked either unpleasant associations or pleasant associations currently unattainable. At some point I recalled a cassette tape someone shared with me back when cassettes were top of the pile. In an instance that is becoming ever more common, I cannot find the cassette, nor can I remember who gave me the cassette or where or when. Instead of a specific memory, there is just a thin cloud of free-associating threads: working at the roller skating rink, song titles scrawled in ballpoint pen on the cassette label, some possible Van Halen on Side A or was it Ozzy Osbourne, a song with a pulsing interstellar beat that brought to mind images of passing through galaxies but wasn't Pink Floyd, and images of myself wearing parachute pants, never a good idea, not even back when they fit.

I googled around for a while and never did figure out what the song was. Instead—algorithms ruling all—I wound up streaming Ambient Space Soundscapes.

Before we go any further, I am tempted to apologize to massage therapists for my opening line as it perpetuates a specific stereotype, except that I meant it. Part of the reason this atmospheric music has played so well for me this week is because it quite literally evokes those professional sessions in which I have been treated to not just an hour of de-knotting, but an hour in which the stillness and darkness combined with a celestial wash of sound allowed me to detach from all the things that put the knots there in the first place as I sank my face into the cushioned donut and flowed into a deep state of relaxation, or a state of what my brother the logger (yes, loggers get massages too) calls feeling like you could "drool in a bucket." While that last phrase may never make it into their professional crest (What's Latin for "drool"?) (Note if you *do* add it to the crest, please clear it through the proper channels as my brother holds rights to the phrase, and you really don't want to commit copyright infringement against a guy with six chainsaws and a tendency to enjoy being left alone.), your finer massage therapists are doing work both physical and profound.

Beyond the memories it evokes, this music does two things for me: It stretches time and takes my mind along. I admit this may not be helpful if you work on a sawmill or perform neurosurgery, but in my case as I am self-employed in a small room by myself for long stretches of time and prone to burrowing into the center of every dark little problem, it doesn't hurt to have a bunch of synthesizers fake out my head and take it on a free-floating tour of an imaginary cosmos. Whether it's doing some typing for hire or sorting tools in the pole barn, I can find the groove, surface twenty minutes or two hours later, and the mind ride has gone on uninterrupted because so does the cosmos and this music made to evoke it. When my head returns to earth there is still trouble there, but at least the chores are done.

BEANS

LAST NIGHT I STAYED UP UNTIL MIDNIGHT shucking beans. Lest this sound selfless I should report that there was a football game on for most of the session, and shucking beans requires a minimum of attention, allowing me to gather up our humble harvest while yelling at millionaires.

In fact I didn't yell, because while it was a terrific game decided in the literal last second, my chosen team wasn't playing and therefore I was less invested than I had been earlier in the day when I began my bean-shucking shift during the third quarter of the Packers game, which they were winning handily but imperfectly. "You gotta *catch* that!" I hollered, and then spilled the beans, an irony bringing into question my right to question.

My relationship with professional sports—most specifically football—is ambivalent in that I believe they are financially and culturally overvalued to an absurd extent, and yet if you can do the job you should get paid market rate and man I love watchin' them Packers. Our indulgent joys cannot always withstand critical review, and that's pretty much the point.

There is the question of whether or not it would just be cheaper to buy a big bag of beans, but this too is an oversimplification placing too much emphasis on calculations devoid of nuance as it relates to how them beans taste if you remember how sore your thumbs were by the time you split the last husk. I also enjoy stepping outside at halftime to pour beans back and forth between tubs while the wind whisks the chaff clear. If only sifting the detritus from my own existence was so simple. How satisfying it is to pour the clean beans into a glass jar, where they shine like an earth-toned collection of unstrung beads.

Back to the sports and my millionaire comment, once you dig in, you discover the numbers aren't that simple, and every time I hear the term "pampered athletes" deployed in the derogatory, I wonder exactly how many pushups I would be willing to do (and how many doughnuts I would deny) in order to develop a cut to my triceps that could be used to slice cheese, never mind every other mental and physical commitment it takes to make the field at that level. The phrase *shut up and play* suggests a sense of ownership that is delusional at best and wishful at worst.

By my freshman year in college I knew I had played my final football game. (I did harbor the fantasy that I was an undiscovered placekicking prodigy until one day in my early 30s when I went to the local high school field and actually tried to kick a field goal—the results indicated I should probably run right back home and write a book or something.) I have often overestimated my talents, and even more so my importance. As antidote to this tendency, yesterday between games and bean shifts, my wife and I took a walk out back and down through the valley. The landscape shrunk me, as it does and as it should. The sumac have gone a saturated scarlet and the first yellow birch leaves have dropped in a scatter across the lawn. These things would have happened even had I not reported them.

Michael Perry

ONE MORE APPLE TREE

THE LAND SURROUNDING OUR HOUSE is profuse with apple trees of great variety. Red, green, yellow, and shades between. From crab teensy to fat as a footballer's fist. Slim and sapling, thick and gnarled. I can't speak to their individual provenance. Perhaps they are remnant of old-time orchards, perhaps some of them were planted by birds, maybe some farmer flung a store-bought apple core while resting his plow horse. If I understand geography, history, and myth, Johnny Appleseed did not this way pass, so it wasn't him. Whatever the source, they grow wild all around the place, and even in years when we gather them up for cider and sauce and pies and dehydrate them by the bag and invite friends and family to pick, the harvest doesn't even register as a percentage.

Silly, then, that we'd plant an apple tree on purpose, but we did. When my wife and I pruned it this year in that uncertain season between late winter and early spring, we discussed how long ago we stuck it in the ground and settled on somewhere around seven years. As best we can recall we got it along with a batch of blueberry bushes.

For the first few turns around the sun, we surrounded the sprout with chicken wire, as the local deer have proven time and time again that despite the thousands of acres of forest and farmland surrounding our yard, they follow their cud-cutting snoots on a beeline to our beans, lettuce, hostas, and any number of domesticated edibles visible from the bathroom window, from which I have been known to berate them from a sitting position. I apologize for the image but can report despite a lack of eyebrows, deer can express bemusement.

The tree has now reached a height and size that we've pulled the posts and wire, but the preventive fencing proved prescient, as the minute a leaf protruded through the fence the deer gnawed it off. Even now, while we prune the top and sides, the base branches are snipped on a dead level equivalent to the reach of a whitetail's neck. They are doe-eyed freeloaders and fawning opportunists.

This year's pruning paid off. Not only are the boughs developing a pleasing bonsai shape, the apples are running larger than usual but remain rock solid, snap-crackle crisp, and sweet in a way that causes you to make noises when that first bite hits. The tree is straight organic—we don't use any sprays or powders—and as a result its fruits are uneven, occasionally scabbed, and often contain worms, but they are organic worms and you just eat around them, and furthermore, see the previous sentence.

The tree stands at the top of a slope up which I run wind sprints during bouts of intermittent fitness. For the past week I have used its apples as a carrot, allowing myself to pick and eat one upon completion of the final interval. The skin cracks, the flavor hits, and may I never become jaded to the joy of snatching succulence straight out of the air while strolling through my own backyard. As far as eating around worms to get at the sweetness, I trust you'll work the metaphor based on your own needs and capacity.

Truck Bed Trailer

We have parked the pumpkins in the sun so they may cure. They—along with a winter's-worth of squash and a handful of gourds—are in the truck-bed trailer that came with the farm.

You don't see so many truck-bed trailers these days. (Side note: Some day I will hire a statistician and a graphic artist, and we'll whip up a neat chart diagramming the exponential increase in usage of the phrase "*these days*" as it correlates to age. Just running the numbers on a napkin, I'd say each additional year lived past 40 doubles one's tendency to invoke them. I envision subcategories and crosstabs breaking down additional data points such as: location when uttered ["porch" and "recliner" gonna rank right up there], associated physical manifestations ["shaking head mournfully, lips pursed"], and odds you mutter them while surrounded by people younger than you enjoying themselves.)

We were talking about the trailer. Used to be a time when we ran pickup trucks into the ground then detached the cab, driveshaft, engine, and front wheels. This left the bed, rear wheels, and frame. Then, using a cutting torch and welder (and probably a come-along, a cheater bar, and some swears), we trimmed and bent the frame in a manner allowing the front end of the rails to be pinched together until they formed a triangle set to receive a hitch coupler. This is a simple overview, and use of the term "we" should in no way imply I ever did it myself, although I did fit ours with a wheeled trailer tongue jack after the fact, and it has really saved my back.

I wonder sometimes about the provenance of this old trailer. If it arrived on the property as a shiny new truck that put in its time in service to the family who last farmed here. If it made runs to town for feed and salt blocks and maybe broke the speed limit a tad when the folks were trying to make kickoff at the high school football game after hustling through the milking chores. Or if it went on any dates or hosted a first kiss. Many of us country kids of certain vintage found our first romance in farm trucks, had our first breakups in farm trucks, and learned early how picking someone up for a date in a farm truck served as a screening mechanism of sorts, as only those partners imbued with a certain laissez-faire hardiness and possibly impaired sense of smell showed for a second date.

I wonder too about the truck's final day of service. Of what happened that the owner finally shook his or her head and said, *Yep, it's time to chop 'er.* Did it blow a rod? Did the floor rust through? Did the kid ram it into a light pole while looking into the eyes of his homecoming date?

These days (there it is again!) the ethos of lease and trade-in and financing and whatnot has reduced the number of trucks driven to their graves, let alone repurposed as trailers. To put it another way, rarely do we finish a vehicle off, unlike my brother John, who, after dragging my father's Ford F-100 to the back forty scrap heap after it was finally wrecked and rusted beyond resurrection, shot it in the radiator purely out of respect.

We've used our truck bed trailer to haul firewood, pole barn junk, giggling city kids, and this year, a portion of the harvest, currently curing in the sun. A nod then, to whoever it was back in those days who built us a cart for these days.

Blue Tarp

For the past three days the wind has swept every loose object in the yard stage left as framed by the window of my little room above the garage. Empty feed bags, cardboard boxes left over from the final potato dig, an empty five-gallon bucket, a blue tarp plastered against the frost-scorched peonies at the base of the flagpole. Even the chickens huddle up, pressed against the weedy tree line like a flock of feathered tumbleweeds.

I am aware of the privilege inherent in staring out my own window. This has not been an easy stretch, but I know better than to complain when I can just slide a sash up to sniff a fresh-blown gust or, better yet, step outside into a situation of social distancing best expressed in terms of acres. I just got off the phone with a family member about to report to a job in health care where she will serve in a setting far less benign than it once was. Now when I step out the door into the pushy air and listen to it heave and sigh and surge through the needles of the bordering Norway pines or hiss through the whippier stripped maple standing solo between me and the house, I salute the wind for what it is: a purification.

Despite the loose items cited above, we're in pretty good shape, fall cleaning-wise. The garden fences, stakes, posts, trellises (trellii?), tomato frames, and assorted hand implements are gathered up and stored for the winter. We still have a few rich rows of kale and chard standing, and they must be good, because yesterday in the bright sunlight of midafternoon we had to chase a pair of deer off them. We were going to plant the garlic last weekend, but the soil was straight dust and hardpack from the recent drought, so I unrolled all the soaker hoses I'd carefully stowed in the pole barn and softened up the patch overnight only to have it rain the following morning despite what my phone told me (in my youth we relied on a weather app called The Old Norwegian Farmer Up The Road) so now I get to re-roll a set of mud-caked hoses, but this is a small price to pay for garlic cloves the size of orange slices. To say nothing of the invigorating sight of those green spikes piercing the snow next spring.

Ah, but there is much to navigate between then and now. We are winding up a year of tumult and unease with no clear finish line. Sometimes homilies won't do, and I am not going to cast current events as some metaphorical blessing when they have been quite the opposite experience for millions. There is a rattle in the air, the leaves doing their scatter-dance across the driveway, the last moment of freedom for a leaf, the one chance to make a break for it before stopping and settling to wait for decay. Or maybe, just maybe, there comes a wind of change, a fresh puff that puts them once more to wing, back toward the tree from which they fell.

FROST

THE MORNING AIR WAS DEAD STILL. Every fallen leaf, every blade of grass, every shingle in sight was furred with frost. Down-valley, a column of smoke from the neighbor's wood boiler rose briefly, its climb to the sky capped by a fixed thermal layer that leveled it off dead square, then smeared it flatly sideways.

There is a term—ekphrasis—that I do not fully grasp but understand in general to mean the vivid and specific description of whatever it is the writer observes. In modern times, ekphrasis has come to more specifically refer to the description of a work of art, but when faced with a frosty morning, let's go with the ancients, who included any thing or any experience. When attempting odes in rural Wisconsin, the poet will find that Grecian urns are in short supply. Expedience may dictate a contemplation upon the plastic five-gallon bucket with *VENISON* scrawled upon it in Sharpie.

I may have first encountered the term ekphrasis in reference to the poetry of Mark Doty, a man known for his close study of objects. In a 2012 interview with the *Kenyon Review*, Doty said ekphrastic writing becomes "a touchstone for meditation." That's nice. It was calming to step into the crystal-muffled silence of the morning and draw clean air while admiring smoke and then attempt to recreate the scene here at the keyboard. It was a cheat code for peace.

But Doty also knows there are limits to committing ekphrasis solely for yourself. In the same *Kenyon Review* piece Doty said, "I would hazard that good ekphrastic writing says *I'm here, you're there*, whereas the weaker stuff says *here we are."* I like this. Rather than heightening our separation, it draws on it as a means of pinpointing where our different perspectives intersect. You don't need me to tell you what smoke on a still, chill morning looks like. But if through that attempt at description our minds' eyes meet somewhere in the neurogenic atmosphere, well, that's us visiting each other on a quiet morning in the country, right this very second.

Once the chickens were fed, I drove the youngster to town for school. Unprompted by her maudlin and ekphratic father, she remarked on the beauty of the frosty landscape and an unusual cloud formation off to the east. These moments seem ever more delicately fixed in time for a multitude of reasons, be it current events, the impending teenage years, or the first big snowstorm due to blow in later today. It is easy to overdo the dad jib-jab, so I just smiled into the rear-view mirror and let the moment ride. Soon enough we would be back to chores, homework, and K-pop. For now we had a rolling view to the country from our old van, my outer calm and easy smile camouflaging a fervent hope that the child might commit her own ekphrasis to heart, that she might contain this vision long after the frost crystal shatters, melts, or evaporates, gone to take a different form in a different time.

Unguarded

Last week i happened across a friend's name in a most unexpected context, specifically plop in the middle of a *New Yorker* article. The article was about politics, and my friend manifested in the form of what I think you might call an indirect quote of an indirect quote or perhaps the second cousin of an indirect quote, but then I'm not your local grammar expert, as readers occasionally point out. Point is, a leading figure discussing one of the prime white-hot neighbor-splitting issues of the day dropped my pal's name in there, so I shot him a text and congratulated him for getting into the *New Yorker* before I.

In response, he texted, "Wait, what?!?!"

That right there is a *direct* quote.

After he read the piece, we ended up on the phone. Turns out he has a relative in the politics business who referenced my friend as a means of imparting "common man" context to the mood of the general populace.

Which my friend would rather he had not.

Especially since the result was—ironically enough—short on context.

We can let that go for now. Upshot is, the whole thing led to us having a fine catch-up conversation. The two of us live several states apart. We see each other maybe once every year or two, in a friendship that probably qualifies half a notch above acquaintances. But wow, was it good to talk.

As it turns out we were both alarmed, mystified, grumpy, and a few other descriptors regarding the state of things in general. With a 93% overlap in perspective. So we really let 'er rip.

There's a lot of talk about making sure we maintain conversation across the fences that divide us, and I second that with all my fraidy-cat heart, even as I falter. The French philosopher and essayist Montaigne warned us against only ever speaking to those with whom we agree, which he described (indirect quote alert) as following the flow of traffic on the same path as those whose opinions cause us to nod and say, "Ah, that is so."

By very virtue of birth, neighborhood, and geography, I am spared treading water in the thin broth of a single opinion whether I fancy it or not, and I figure that's strengthening.

And yet: Sometimes you need a conversation without guardrails. Time on the phone, or around the fire, or at the mailbox, or wherever time, trust, and privacy allow—to just let it all pour out, to speak without fault or favor, to spend more time nodding than gritting your teeth. Some call it self-care. Some call it blowing off steam. I'm just glad I called.

There is a corollary in parenting: Anyone fortunate enough to have shared the privilege of raising children with a good partner knows there are times when the two of you need to meet up and trip the ol' pressure relief valve and rattle off every character flaw, every maddening habit, every reason the kid is never gonna find the laundry basket let alone success in this world, so that you can then draw a deep cleansing breath and go back to loving that child in the way you never stopped loving that child.

See y'down the road.

Deadlift

Typing up this weekly dispatch is not a difficult job, and I am daily grateful for it, but the chronological logistics do present certain boutique challenges. For instance, the deadline for this piece predates the election results, meaning I either make a daring prediction (I am neither willing nor qualified) or compose some innocuous pablum designed to play either way.

For those of you wishing to exercise your critical chops, I offer the phrase "innocuous pablum" as a fat softball floated directly across home plate. Have at 'er.

No matter what happens at the ballot box (and I respectfully include any serious developments or unforeseen side effects), it seems safe to say garlic and human goofiness will survive, so those are the threads I shall pursue.

Regarding goofiness, it's tough to know where to begin, but my recent commitment to makeshift deadlifting seems a fine place to start.

While I am in fact and by definition engaging in deadlifting every time I hoist my hinder off the couch while the commercials roll during a Packers game, that probably doesn't count. I refer instead to the weight training exercise currently back in vogue with a wide range of folks, including the mathematical statistician and essayist Nassim Nicholas Taleb, who leverages the concept of risk management and complexity theory to cast deadlifting as a route to robustness and antifragility. Taleb has written and even Tweeted of this at length, and I really don't understand how it all ties into his overall theories, but it did make sense that perhaps at my age it would be good to continue lifting heavy things as long as I can and thus extend my capacity for same.

Apart from a couple of dusty barbells that emit guilt rays from a corner of my office, I haven't done any serious weightlifting since college when I went through a phase of subscribing to bodybuilding magazines with names like *Flex* and went to the gym mainly to admire the mirror. These days I don't possess a proper deadlift setup. In fact I don't have a weightlifting set at all, at least not the kind with a knurled bar and fat do-nut-holed plates. I did a quick online search, but it turns out—and I am not kidding—the pandemic has resulted in a shortage of weightlifting equipment.

And so it is you will find me three times a week down in the pole barn wearing fleece-lined leather work gloves and deadlifting a steel fence post threaded through two concrete blocks. It's a crude setup and not the sort of thing to land you on the cover of *Flex*. Still, after just a few weeks, my back feels sturdier, I've increased both my reps and sets, and I'm set to add a couple more bricks.

On what might seem an unrelated note, the garlic is bedded, mulched, and sitting there waiting for spring. This always gives me a measure of peace as we go into winter. Garlic is patient and survives being left out in the cold. Meanwhile, we do our heavy lifting, preparing for more heavy lifting.

Tomatoes

This year's final batch of tomatoes is slow-bubbling in the stock pot. Out there in the dark, a steady November rain is chilling the earth. This closes the circle nicely, as just six months ago our little family of four got soaked to the shorts transplanting the last of the tomato plants in an utter monsoon. It was a character-building experience, or so I shall describe it in my memoirs. I cannot vouch for how my children shall describe it in theirs.

Those tomatoes we transplanted were plastered flat the following morning, but you wouldn't have known it when harvest time arrived. Over the course of the summer they jungled up in profusion. In addition to the long rows planted intentionally, a big cluster of volunteers sprang up in the previous year's plot. We gathered them by the bucket and box, tomatoes of every shape, consistency, and color, from mottled green to bright yellow to deep, deep red. Even with friends and relatives helping out and lightening the load, we could barely keep up. The reducing and canning and freezing went on and on.

And then the culmination: my wife and me in the kitchen, chunking up the final collection.

It is tricky to second-guess one's life partner, especially in matters of food preservation. But I gotta tell ya: I dragged my feet on this last batch.

My wife is the prime catalyst behind our gardening endeavors, and our grocery budget benefits because of it. The savings factor is multiplied by her deeply ingrained resistance to waste. This is reminiscent of my own mother, who among other things was known to spoon spilt milk back into the pitcher, repurpose food from the local jail, and raised a huge and healthy passel of kids on expired goods and dented cans. I'm not saying Mom ever uttered the phrase, "You can just eat around that," but I maintain it was implied. On a related note, if your wife commits an act of economy that reminds you of your mom, noting so by calling your wife your mother's name prefaced by "OK there," may earn you some real cold alone time.

The point is, these final tomatoes had been plucked before the big frost and left to allegedly ripen; in fact they looked like the nightshades section of a plant diseases and disorders handbook. There was wizening, deformity, odd spots, frank rot, and general squishiness.

Timidly I broached the idea that perhaps we would make it through the winter without them.

What my wife said in response is irrelevant; I got to chopping, trimming, and excising. When it was all over I'd say we ran a ratio of roughly 2:1 stock pot to chicken bucket, but I was done broaching and instead will just say that we are good on tomatoes this year.

At one point near the end I noticed my wife was not working as surgically as I, and in fact was tossing in product not up to my standards. Reading my face, she smiled brightly and said, "Oh you'd be surprised the things you eat that you don't know about," and I will think about that all winter long.

SANDHILL CRANES

I HEARD THE CRANES before I saw them, high as they were in the sky, pale sandhills strung loosely across the blue, their wings underlit by the late afternoon sun, each a soft strobe as it flapped. This being a time of uncertainty I took the sight of them in migration as comfort in the form of a cycle preserved. There was also the metaphor of them flying high above it all, lucky birds.

Poetics have their limits, and in fact here on the ground other things required my attention. The new aluminum ladder has reemerged from the last snow and must be stowed. The chicken coop must be moved uphill to where the extension cord will reach it so I can plug in the heated watering bucket—already most mornings the unheated version cradles a disc of ice. Out along the fencerow there is one more pile of oak to split and stack before it's socked in snow.

Yesterday I spent an hour on the phone with a friend who lost his father to the coronavirus. Sixty years old and gone. One story among thousands, and thousands more by now. Our collective reaction to the pandemic has been the confounding experience of my life. Just today I heard the phrase, "Well, she was in her 80s," as if somehow this was mitigation. I've been preparing to die for decades now and operate somewhere between pragmatism and self-preservation but hope I have never slipped into flippancy regarding my mortality, let alone that of another human being.

There is also the reality that ranks of health care professionals are pulling understaffed overtime shifts in the face of this beast. I volunteer on a regional hospital board. This week facilities were at 100% capacity, and scores of staff were sidelined due to exposure.

When it comes to standing atop soapboxes, my sense of balance is tenuous. I am uncomfortable up there and easily toppled. Furthermore, even as I speak, my own failings heckle me from ground level. So to be clear: I am not impervious to stumbles and poor judgment. I have commitments in the next 48 hours for which the risk is near-zero but not zero. But I'll keep masking up and hope you will too. This is mitigation in the mathematical sense. It won't take us to zero, but it'll help us trend that way as we await the cavalry.

Every word I type here is submitted with deference to those enduring the very real pain of social deprivation and economic hardship. As with most euphemisms, neither phrase conveys the gut-punch of reality. I also acknowledge those folks working because we have deemed them essential, or their own economic survival demands it. We can do more to help them.

I am in over my head, and you didn't hire me to tell you how to live. From my desk I can see chickens working the green grass of the yard while it's still available. In general they move as a flock, but there are intermittent tussles and peck-fests. If sandhill cranes are anything like chickens, I suppose they don't always live in harmony either, but at least twice a year they manage to get it together to fly in the same direction.

Deer Hunting

Down in the valley I hear the end of day unfold from a distance. The rooster is crowing. He needn't, as he has crowed the sun up and now nearly down to the horizon, but then anyone who has ever owned or lived in proximity to one knows a rooster crowing at dawn is but warming up for a series of daylong self-congratulatory hoots, and we aren't even addressing clear nights with a full moon.

Rooster does as roosters do, but a more rhythmic sound is also echoing from the hills above me: the *chunk-clunk* of firewood hitting the bottom of a cart. This means my younger daughter is doing at least one of her chores. Soon the percussion is joined by melody. I can't make out words, but it is her voice, pealing out in song. This does not mean she is happy doing the chore, but that she has learned to pass the time while doing the chore.

Three days now I have been up before first light to sit in the woods, not that you'd know it to check my freezer. I have spent an hour watching a great gray owl with its head on a swivel scanning the swamp grass for rodents. I have watched a weasel flowing bright white over deadfalls and brown leaves. I have listened to crows rattle and caw. I have not taken a deer.

The week leading up to deer season was windy; the past three days have been largely dead calm. I am closing out this day in a stand of Norway pines. The ground is blanketed in rust-orange needles; they dampen and deepen the stillness. From forty feet away I can hear a chickadee's pencil-point talon scratching the bark.

The sun is laying its last light on the land with a low-angle intensity. The shadows are long and growing longer, but the southwest-facing tree trunks are white-bright, and common patches of brush are transformed into a gilded latticework. As with any star, the sun hits you with its most artistic licks just before the curtain drops.

It happens this patch of land is in the government's Managed Forest Law program. Many of the trees around me are marked for harvest, the blaze orange spray paint the only unnatural element in sight. I wonder what this woodlot will look like in a year. It occurs to me that already some logger somewhere has prepared the bid that will win the job, and I am looking at his family's grocery money. It also occurs to me that somewhere some pulpwood futures trader is living off these trees even as they stand awaiting the blade. It is possible the trader doesn't know a raker from a cutter, but he will wind up with more grocery money than the logger.

I am off on this tangent when I notice movement to my left. A deer butt, disappearing. So it goes. Yesterday I sat in a blind for five hours, and when I opened the flap to go for lunch, a whitetail bolted snorting from just behind me. It popped over the ridge but then stopped just out of sight and blew at me derisively. A day later it's a different deer, same result. Dusk has arrived, and I hike up the hill, eager to see the lit windows of my home, warm inside, with stacked firewood and song to keep it so.

Not a Pig Farmer

As someone who types for a living, it pains me to repeat this old saw, but: You shouldn't believe everything you read, especially the Wikipedia entry that as of today says I am a pig farmer.

This raises the fair question of why I am reading my own Wikipedia entry. The answer lies somewhere between vanity and fear and checking to see if whoever is in charge of these things has added my latest book, which they have not. I'll ask to speak to the manager.

The rest of the material is accurate enough and comprising but a few brief lines. The brevity is in fact a relief. Serenity is tied in part to remaining largely overlooked. And as inaccuracies go, "pig farmer" is an honorific.

In fact the erroneous bio is self-imposed. For a while, I did raise pigs. And blabbed about it publicly. But at its peak the herd topped out at five, and most years was but a pair. (An aside: The *Old Farmers Almanac* refers to a group of pigs variously as a drift, a drove, a passel, a team, and a sounder; the Wikipedia "pig" entry contains none of this poetry.)

In print and in public I pointedly referred to myself as an "amateur" pig farmer; that is to say, a writer with some pigs. At best it was a boutique side gig; if the porkers flopped over dead or escaped to Minnesota while I was on book tour, it wasn't the end of my livelihood, and I acknowledged that. Real farming is difficult enough without public pretenders.

Later, after several consecutive years passed with the pig pen empty, I began referring to myself as an "intermittent" pig farmer but eventually dropped even that wiggle room as it implied the pigs would return, and while I hold out hope, all signs point to nope. At this point I'm down to a motley flock of chickens. They did not make the Wikipedia page and are frankly wrankled.

I am of rural stock, a boots-and-pitchfork boy, but neither my flock nor my passel qualify me to claim the farmer mantle. Also, plenty of city folk keep chickens. But it's good to have a few daily chores, something to keep me tethered to the land and its cycles. Something that preempts my own priorities. To start the day by pouring feed and water for the critters before downing my coffee and eggs. In the cowboy books I read as a child, the good guy who came in starving from the trail never ate his beans until he'd fed and watered his horse. It's a modest but noble responsibility.

Pigs? Perhaps again one day. Until such time, among other things not reported in Wikipedia, tonight when I crossed the yard as a defunct dilettante swineherd bound to close up the chicken coop, the full moon illuminated a thin sweep of cloud positioned just so that it appeared Orion was clad in a toga. "Huh!" I said, addressing the universe out loud, as we sometimes do.

Humility

HUMILITY CAN BE CULTIVATED OR IMPOSED. Today we will speak of the latter.

I have long said I prefer to run close to the dirt as eventually we all fall, and why not minimize the drop? This requires humility in word, action, and comportment—not necessarily the most popular move in this the age of self-promoting go-getters.

At this juncture it is fair to point out I have more than one social media account set up for the sole purpose of self-promotional go-getting. It is also fair to observe that he who writes of humility and submits that writing for publication is at some level sending mixed messages.

So much for cultivation. Let us switch to imposition. To humility served right to your face. Spoon-fed if you're fortunate, but sometimes by the shovelful. And delivered—as with the two anecdotes to follow—in the form of friendly fire.

As it happens, both incidents involve music. My music. The music I humbly compose and humbly play and less-than-humbly self-promote. One needs to feed the band.

The band in question comprises true professionals save one: Me. The other members have long honed their craft; I am a late-arriving four-chord clammer. Everyone in the ensemble (including me) acknowledges that I have every honest reason to remain humble about my musicianship. Never was this more succinctly put than during preparations for our last pre-pandemic show: While sorting out the stage plot and plug-ins, a new sound tech not familiar with my skills asked my pal and band director Evan, "Does Mike play guitar?"

Without hesitation and within earshot, Evan replied, "Mike *has* a guitar..."

As he spoke the words his face was lit with evil delight. There were guffaws all around.

Fast forward to last night. I've composed a new song. The band and I have recorded it, a videographer and I have shot a video to accompany it, and I am reviewing the work on our living room flat screen. My wife and younger daughter have joined me. I turn the volume up, and we are halfway through the second pass when there comes a thudding in the hallway from above, and shortly my elder daughter emerges at the base of the stairs with a look like someone spoilt her soup, and says, "What is this heinous music you're playing?"

The duality of parenting imbues us with the ability to love the child who so humbles us; it also imbues us with the ability to flip the script in an instant. Rather than flop to frown or purse in a pout, my face lit up, mirroring my pal Evan's evil delight, because in the split-second instant after her question hung in the air and before she realized who was singing, I realized I was going to be able to hang this one over her head in perpetuity.

"It's my new song," I said.

Reader, she hit reverse so fast it stripped her gears, and she just spun. We laughed and laughed. The three of us, and then the four of us. Humility for two, joy for all.

           Michael Perry

Dry Ice

THIS WEEK I WAS INCLUDED in a group email passed down from a state government employee to a county-level employee and finally shared by a deputy in one of our local fire departments. Attached was a paper composed by the International Association of Fire Chiefs detailing the proper response to emergency incidents involving dry ice.

The paper was informative and straightforward, and the recommended field procedures equally so, but it was good to have a refresher. I read it beginning to end.

Bureaucratic overkill drives even the gentlest of us over the foaming edge. I myself may have just this week engaged in a parking lot rant borne of the imperfect intersection of government paperwork and technology... thankfully I was locked inside my own van at the time. It would be tempting to view updates on dry ice emergencies as an overwrought take on the mundane. Shoot, grandpa used to buy the stuff at Canadian gas stations and pack it around walleye filets in a Styrofoam cooler.

And yet my first thought at receiving the dry ice email was that it represented the responsible work of conscientious stewards of incremental civility, expressed in this instance through forward-looking concern for the safety of citizens and first responders. When I heard news of the first vaccines being released against this pandemic, I knew some would need to be packed in dry ice; what I didn't extrapolate was that this—as the IAFC alert put it—would result in "unprecedented creation, movement, and storage of these materials." In other words, we're gonna fly, truck, and lift a lotta dry ice over the next many months.

Overwhelming odds are: it'll go fine. Dry ice ain't nuclear waste. But neither is it benign should a bunch of it spill and workers or rescuers come in contact with it, or should a container leak in a confined space where the off-gassing carbon dioxide displaces the oxygen. It didn't hurt me to review standard operating procedures and be prepared should the call come in, and it was wise of these folks to put them on my radar.

The subject here isn't centered on long-shot dry ice incidents. It's about public servants who take their jobs seriously. Citizens who tend to the structure of society. Quiet people enacting civilized behavior in times of incivility. County clerks, election officials, the person trying to upgrade the frustrating website on a shoestring budget, good people doing their best within imperfect systems. The last time I went to the much-maligned DMV, I was given a number, served promptly, and the individual behind the counter not only processed my paperwork smoothly, she solved an unanticipated problem right there in the moment. Your mileage may vary—mine has—but what I'm trying to do here is recognize the effort when the effort is sincere, and even more importantly, unheralded.

Lest I hector or come off as pious, I assure you I know what it is to "press" zero on my phone with enough vigor to snap my finger at the knuckle. To retrieve the crumpled tax form from across the room and smooth it on the desk. Just this month, on the fourth try at filling out my livestock premises registration form, I succumbed and left an ALL CAPS snark in the field that wouldn't let me proceed unless I entered information that didn't exist.

But I'm better now. If you're out there doing your part to anticipate trouble so we can ignore it, if you're daily sweeping pebbles from the collective path, if you're quietly tending the foundation while so many yell from the rooftops, thank you.

END OF YEAR

WINTER IS RUNNING LATE. I realize I am speaking only for myself, but so it goes with weather patterns. "In jet streams as with life, we are at the whim of the winds," he wrote, sounding vaguely mystic but mostly obvious. Stitch *that* on a sampler and frame it in plastic.

Atop our specific hill, Santa has come and gone and still the snowplow sits on blocks in the shed. This is tempting fate, but then procrastination is my prime art form, and few modern conveniences enable this more than ready access to the ten-day forecast via the phone in your palm.

Nearly all year long the news in my palm has left me longing for calm. All things are relative, and the list of gratitudes stretches like a Christmas receipt, but this year's not-so-subliminal scroll has been an all-caps COUNT YOUR BLESSINGS AND CHECK YOUR STANDING. Also, LEND A HAND.

Many years ago my elders put me on to the idea of reading history as a means of calibrating my perception of what constitutes a personal drama. I continue this practice as a means of countering egocentric pensiveness. Yesterday's news—be it centuries old—serves as a shock absorber for the soul, or the nightly news, which of course is now the perpetual motion news.

That said, even a passing familiarity with history will attune your soul to echoes that bounce back in the key of dread. The concept of citizenship has fallen under heavy review and revision, and sometimes I don't know how to talk to my neighbors, or if they want to talk to me.

But we do talk. From a distance out by the mailbox, mostly, and oftentimes not about what is prime in our minds, but even speculation about a snowstorm is communication in commonality. Down the hill our neighbors Denny and Linda put up a Christmas display that lifts our hearts every time we drive past it, so my daughters called and told them so. These are the threads we weave in hopes they will hold.

Last night—by electronic means, as is the quarantine norm—I attended a concert by a young singer. She is just into her teens, and sang with a power and purity of someone troubled but not yet cowed by humankind's unkindnesses. In other words, she opened her heart and made her stand. It is tempting to cast this as some year-end wrap, print it out, and stick it on the fridge like a resolution, but instead I choose simply to surf the sweet echo of it, hear it in the key of youth no matter how droopy my ears might be, and look to the future with a freshness I may not feel but am compelled to foster.

New Music

LAST NIGHT WHILE STREAMING MUSIC at random, the algorithm kicked out a song that moved me to hit repeat. After three listens I added it to a list of favorites so it will cycle through again.

This doesn't happen much anymore. A byproduct of aging, I suppose. In youth, the conscious was an uncrowded canvas. We catalogued fresh colors on the daily. Music mediated the emotions we were still coming to know. The songs that struck, stuck.

I am still sustained by music and, sometimes, new music. But the voraciousness of my early days is tempered by a back catalog that already speaks for the majority of my mind spaces and memories. The new stuff has to clear that hurdle.

My teenaged daughter is currently deeply invested in K-Pop. She can discourse on the details of not only the groups and their songs but the names of each individual member and their backstory. She has brought ol' Dad up to speed on terms like "my bias" ("my favorite") and spends hours memorizing and recreating the intricate dance moves associated with the performance of a particular single. She will also speak earnestly and at length about what feels to me like mind-numbing trivia underpinning the genre, but to her is a means of interpreting and framing her world, her culture, and her times.

It is that earnestness I try to honor even if I maintain music peaked the day Waylon Jennings plugged his leather-bound Telecaster into a phase shifter and recorded "Mammas Don't Let Your Babies Grow Up To Be Cowboys." There was a time I believed Waylon Jennings sang my life;

in fact he sang about 12 percent of my life, and the rest was me projecting, dreaming, and generally self-aggrandizing. But he did knock me off the path just enough to nudge me into a trajectory I wouldn't trade for any steadier situation. So it is I smile through the K-Pop disquisitions, hearing with my heart if not my ears.

And, happily, I am still capable of being transported by a tune. Last night it was "The Spark" by William Prince. Coulda been my mood, coulda been the acoustics, coulda been the week in general, but it certainly was also something about the ease and resolution of the lyrics, the phrasing, all the little alchemies of music that transmute sound into spirit.

At a certain age and mileage we have accumulated so many experiences it is nearly impossible for just one song to be *the* song. But music is a marvel of infinite arrangements, and I like the idea of my young daughter in her upstairs bedroom, surrounded by posters of her chosen popsters, working out her lexicon of living, the music suffusing and shaping her as no music may ever do again, and meanwhile her old dad out here working in a little room above the garage, unlikely to bust moves or rave or tape a poster to the wall but able still to feel a song in his soul, and in such a way that he may remain open to the joyous obsessions of youth.

Ice Skating

There's a spring-fed pond way out back that's perfect for skating because if you break through you'll at worst get your ankles muddy. In drier years there is no pond at all by fall, but this year after a solid winter freeze, a sizeable patch of ice remained, and yesterday my younger daughter asked if I would chauffeur her and a classmate out for a skate.

My first reaction was the usual deskbound harrumphing: no time... can't possibly...deadlines...getting the taxes together...blather-blather, etc., and then, like someone took to my wooden head with a rubber mallet, I was struck by a vision of this moment as a dot along the number line of time.

Sure, I said. Get the hot chocolate ready.

When the classmate arrived, I started our old plow truck and fetched a bucket of kindling and firewood, a snow shovel and a pair of camp chairs. Both families have been navigating strict quarantine routines over the holidays, so rather than pack into the cab, the two of them rode in the back of the truck as I bumped slowly out the trail. When I checked the mirror they were chattering behind their masks, the cloth doing double duty in these cold pandemical times, and reminding me that this skating session was critical for them on many levels.

All my amateur psychoanalyses tend toward overcomplicating the obvious, so forthwith, a simpler report: Upon reaching the farthest reaches of the farthest-back forty, we gathered up our gear and hiked down a steep footpath to a valley and the pond. While the girls donned their skates, I shoveled an oblong track through the accumulated snow.

The ice beneath was off-and-on smooth and nubby.

As the skaters took their first turn (giggling when they hit the teeth-chattering nubby stretch), I gathered twigs and canary grass and coaxed up a fire ("coaxed" being a euphemism for blazing up a dozen wooden matches and a brace of kindling stolen from the household stash). By the time the fire caught, the two friends were making snow angels and ready for their first hot chocolate break.

At this point I figured the old guy might harsh the middle-school vibe, so I set out for a walk, leaving them in their camp chairs trying to avoid the smoke from my sad fire while drinking hot chocolate. My daughter had also produced a bag of corn chips coated in blaze orange cheese dust, perhaps to counterbalance all the nature.

I walked without purpose, and was that ever long overdue. I wound up following the spring to its source. In its final approach to the pond, it seeps and dissipates through a marsh and is essentially invisible. But as I climbed ever deeper up the cut from which it emanates, the click and chuckle of flowing water grew. Then, at a point where several deer tracks converged, I spotted an opening roughly the size of a whitetail's snoot, through which a wrist-thick braid of water flowed over a bed of black and white sand.

Then I heard, "Dad?" from downvalley, my daughter's voice raised just enough to carry, and of a tone a father recognizes not as an emergency but as, "We're cold and ready to go."

I covered the coals with snow, and we climbed out to the truck. Within the hour I was back at the desk, swept not with any fresh resolve or illuminating epiphany, simply back to chasing deductions, but echoing with the skate-blade scrape, youth's laughter from a distance, and the idea of a world laced with invisible springs.

Woodshed Doors

Who knows what transpired in the last twenty-four hours let alone twenty minutes, but right now I'm grateful to my father for the trees he felled on his farm and had sawn into the boards that now form our woodshed doors.

We wouldn't have that woodshed in the first place if not for my father, who not only helped me build it, he has often helped me fill it. In fact, just last fall he and my mother drove down on a couple of occasions to cut and stack firewood with us. They will both turn 80 this year, but when I demurred they wouldn't hear it. In short, after a life spent farming and logging for a living, Dad assures me he enjoys running his chainsaw as a form of recreation and that it feels different to do it as a favor rather than as a form of financial survival. Which is to say, these days we kids are by and large feeding ourselves.

Although some of us still welcome help catching up with the wood-making.

So if your father's idea of a busman's holiday is to drop and chop those couple of dead oak trees alongside the driveway, you accept the offer. As it turned out, the day they arrived I had to leave at midmorning and drive to town for my annual physical. When we reached the health history segment and the doctor asked me if both of my parents were still alive, I said yes, and when he asked me how they were doing, I explained that en route to his office I had to steer around the octogenarian pair of them as they moved oak blocks off the drive.

The woodshed is a simple structure and a simple blessing: four walls and a roof to keep the rain and snow off the stacks, with three doorways for easy access. Until recently, however, the doorways lacked doors. This critical last step in the project had been delayed due to lack of hardware, and before you know it I'd been "gonna get to that" for several years. So before Dad came down to make firewood again, I measured the openings, and he precut a batch of one-inch planks selected from his "economy" lumber stash, which is good enough for woodshed doors and children with poor follow-through.

But I did it. Got the hardware, got out the sawhorses, built the doors, and hung 'em. Rough-cut boards, rough-cut results. Some gaps, but that's OK in a woodshed. Hardly finish carpentry. Hung one door backward and had to undo it all. But how lovely it is to swing each door smoothly closed, drop the hook-and-eye latch in place, and know the wood will be dry and ready when the storm passes.

This morning I paused along the path to the chicken coop and took a photo of the woodshed so Dad can see the doors in place. How lovely it will be to tromp out after the next blizzard, pull open those doors, and see the wood, stacked and dry. How grateful I am for my parents. How I wish the world held more like them. How I wish a simple homemade door was enough to protect all precious things.

Michael Perry

The Descent

A LONG TIME AGO I USED TO RACE BICYCLES. Long enough ago that when I tucked into a descent, my hair flowed out from beneath my helmet and snapped like ribbons in the wind. Now it's been decades since my hair flowed anywhere but down the shower drain.

Last night I got a text out of the blue from a friend from those racing days, someone I accrued a few thousand pedal-powered miles with over the years. We'll call him Speed.

I was a solid middle-of-the-pack cyclist with a few top-ten finishes on an extremely regional circuit; Speed was a champion and even pulled a brief stint as a pro.

Following Speed's rear tire for a few thousand miles over the years, I had plenty of time to ponder the difference between our levels of achievement; the distinction came down to genes and fearlessness.

Work ethic? I had it. When Speed lured me into a pell-mell 114-mile training ride through the Mississippi hills after less than two weeks of training, I didn't quit. I ground away until—well after dark, dehydrated, and nutritionally concussed—I was back in my apartment and unable to do anything other than stiff-leg it to my mattress, tip over backward, and not move.

Train as I might, I could never out-sprint or out-climb Speed's fast-twitching aerobic machine of a body. But where he really lost me— *dropped me*, in the parlance of the peloton—was at the fear factor. With all the clarity of ten minutes ago, I recall bringing my wrists, elbows, and knees together, raising my rear out of the saddle, projecting my helmeted head well out over the handlebars, and following him into the first asphalt curve on the down-bound side of those Mississippi hills. We wove the first few sweeps smoothly, but already he was pulling away. Air was coursing ever more loudly through my helmet, and I remember a guardrail as a silver blur just off my kneecap. I leaned harder into the turn and checked my speedometer.

57 miles an hour.

Nope.

Gently, gently I touched the brakes and pulled out of my aerodynamic crouch. Speed was gone now, well out of sight. I continued to feather the brakes, but even at a cautious touch I could smell scorch.

Eventually I emerged at the base of the hill, where Speed—just as he did at the crest of long climbs—was circling, waiting for me to rejoin him. Onward we pedaled.

It was good to hear from Speed. He tends to disappear—for years, sometimes—then resurface. It felt odd to relive our sweat-drenched trek through the hills on a random January day nearly three decades after the fact, but come bedtime the memory clarified itself in context: Sometimes after a long, winding slog uphill into the wind for what feels like, oh, four years, you find yourself hurtling down the other side thinking escape velocity is just the thing, but then you sit up and think what would be really nice is a simple ride through the country. Less roller, more coaster.

Forward.

MEMORY POTHOLES

THE ROAD TO AGING GRACEFULLY is filled with potholes, and many of those are filled with nostalgia. For instance, this morning after chicken chores, as I leaned into the teeth of a deep-freeze breeze and my fingers went numb in the time it took to walk from the coop to the porch, I beheld a warm vision of Jerry Coubal spinning the cap off an insulated water jug.

I also had a vision of my mother, asking why I wasn't wearing my mittens.

Jerry was the farmer down the road, and the water jug traveled in the twine box of his John Deere hay baler, behind which I spent many summer afternoons stacking. In that moment after pulling the pin on the loaded wagon and hitching up the empty, we'd gather up and drink. I wrote about it once: "We'd set the cooler on the edge of the empty wagon, unspin the plastic top and turn it over to catch the water from the miniature spigot, then pass it around. I remember raising the water to my lips and seeing bits of chaff skating the surface tension of the water. Our neighbor Jerry would always swirl water in the cap after the last drink, then sling the water to the ground before screwing the cap back on. A little ceremony before we went back to work."

In this morning's moment of freezing fingers, the visual memory of Jerry spinning the cap was accompanied by the sense memory of the sun, the sweat, the alfalfa leaves stuck to my forearms, and even the stillness of the shadowed stubble when the shuttle runner was late with the empty wagon and we lay beneath the shade of the full one, awaiting the sound of the approaching Johnny-Popper.

Thank goodness for these memories. They are mine as long as I can hold them, no matter what happens. They keep me grounded, they sustain my gratitude for the good life I was given. It is tempting to soak in them all day long as a means of easing the creaking bones of present realities. And the muscles I made at that work are still mine.

And there's where I tap the brakes.

Yesterday someone multi-forwarded an email that was essentially a "kids these days" rant. It was mildly heartwarming until it veered off into under-examined self-satisfied hoo-hah regarding the state of things now as opposed to them good old days when stoic souls ruled with firm and judicious hand (but maybe don't check the closet or under the carpet) (parentheses mine). "Today's kids are selfish and spoiled," the email read, as if today's adults were not widely in evidence.

The thing is, there was much to be longed for in that email. The value of honest work and delayed gratification, the best simplicities of times past. I nodded my head more than once and have delivered similar sermons at my own dinner table. How I cherished the presence of seasoned elders like Jerry in my life. But the deeper I read into that email, the less I nodded. "Today's kids rush to the store, buying everything they can...no concern for anyone but themselves," is a snappy line unless you've actually spent ten minutes among the multitudes of young people who are studying, striving, volunteering, and living brightly. Never mind those who have nothing to spend at the store.

I am far too wishy-washy to make a good preacher. I am convulsive in my caveats. I often retreat to the comforts of soft memory in the hard present. It is not mine to give lessons, but it is certainly mine to take them, even those drawn from the young as they observe their elders and form memories of their own.

Award

TODAY AT SUNRISE I received a text from a friend: "Congratulations on your recent award!"

This was news to me, and as does news in general, it made me nervous. Awards news even more so.

Awards invite scrutiny, and scrutiny makes me sweaty. Ironically, I once won an award for a magazine article I wrote about being sweaty. The trophy is propped atop a pole barn girt overlooking my workbench. It is covered in sawdust and needs a polish. Mostly it serves to remind me that I probably shouldn't be playing amateur hour with saws and grinders, as I type for a living and need my fingers.

My editor submitted the sweat essay without my knowledge. This is an important distinction, as the awards of which I shall write today were not awards I sought. They sometimes arrived with prior warning, but I had not placed myself in the pool. (At least not intentionally: It could be said I put myself in the running for the "Biggest Primper" ribbon I received in high school as I had a habit of incessantly feathering my hair. Ultimately graduation and nature rendered me ineligible.)

The poignancy of some awards is based on their inadvertent (and occasionally delayed) power to humble the recipient. I return again to high school where I received the football team's "Most Improved Offensive Lineman" award. I hung that one on the wall and felt pretty good about it until a few years later when I put some distance between me and the glory and did the math required to distill the number of people eligible (three positions out of eleven, drawn from an overall roster numbering twenty-something counting backups and some of them missing practice to help with haying).

If one receives an award without lobbying for it, and it is given purely, it is ungracious to make jokes or self-deprecate to the point of denigrating the folks who took the time to arrange the kindness. Someone had to take me aside and give me a little talk about that once. I think the difficulty is based in knowing myself, my imperfections, how unpolished I am in the day-to-day, how so much of what I do is rooted in uncertainty… there is this awkward feeling that by accepting the award we accept the accolades as gospel revelations.

Ultimately, you try to flip the gratitude. I once received an award from a much-maligned governmental institution and was even sweatier than usual about the whole deal, but the upshot was I was given the opportunity to invite two of the public school teachers who redirected my life for a lifetime to the ceremony and have them stand beside me, and that felt solid and good. As usual, the answer to most self-imposed worry is to seek the path of gratitude. That one's a full-time job.

I will say any time you get an award from librarians you should be very happy and send a handwritten thank-you note. And although I've never been long-listed for any grand literary award, someone once did turn one of my books into a float for the Green County Cheese Days parade, and as I have always said, stick that in your pipe and smoke it, Pulitzer committee.

In the course of wrapping up this column I have received a follow-up text from my friend. It turns out it's not so much an award as a piece selected for a ten-year anniversary project. So no plaque or first class flight to Norway, and no sweating. Instead, it is back to work in gratitude and humility, even if I was once the Most Valuable Player on my high school track team, specifically the year no one else went out for track.

Frozen Pipes

LAST WEEK IN A RARE DEMONSTRATION of foresight and follow-through, having noted a little more light than usual leaking around and through the tattered insulation covering one of our cracked glass block basement windows and with ten days of subzero incoming, I masked up and hit the home improvement store, purchased a single batt of unfaced fiberglass, returned home, and tucked it in and amongst the gaps.

Our basement is damp and dungeon-y in the warm months, dry and dungeon-y in the frozen months. Composed of cobwebs and crawl spaces, it has never been and never will be a "man-cave" basement; it is simply a "cave" basement.

The plumbing is a reflection of the house itself, which originated as a log cabin in the 1880s and was then appended and remodeled by folks who knew how to make things solid but neither level nor square.

Accordingly, water circulates through our house via a mix of old pipes, old copper tubing, new copper tubing (where the old copper tubing failed and the plumber replaced it), and contemporary flexible tubing. The plan has long been to build a new house, so we've never gone in for a total re-plumb. For a number of reasons, the "new house" plan has been annually tabled for numerous consecutive annums, so when I see a long run of negative numbers in the forecast, I always get a little nervous about the pipes. Thirteen years we've lived here, and we've not burst one yet, but time is not on our side.

How good it felt, then, to tuck that fresh insulation in and around the window frame and poke a little here and there in the cracks where the cool air was flowing in fast enough to ruffle my knuckle hair, then step back and look at the work well done. And how *ironic* then, when I went to fill the chicken water bucket in the laundry room the next day only to turn on the faucet and get…nothing.

Thirteen years without a freeze-up and then, within 24 hours of deploying a few ounces of prevention, up it froze. In all our years here we've had far deeper freezes and far longer freezes. I hustled downstairs dreading the sound of spraying water, but thankfully there was no burst, just ice cube blockage.

There followed some creative extension cord routing and space heater hang-and-aim rigging. I also plucked some of the fresh insulation from around the old pipes. What a relief, an hour later, to hear water gushing from the faucet.

Apparently my insulation job rerouted some mini-jet stream that had been flowing harmlessly for years, somehow dropping the temperature where it had not been dropped before.

If the prognosticators have it right, we have another six nights of subzero to go. Before retiring each evening, we set the laundry room and bathroom faucets at a drippy trickle to keep the water in motion, a trick with which anyone who has spent time in old drafty accommodations is well familiar. And the space heaters are in place should it come to that. It is my fervent prayer that when next we convene I will have communed with no plumber.

Antifragile Snowdancer

Last night when I stepped out of the little room over the garage and locked up for the night I heard the sounds of some small creature meeting its end in the forest behind me. There was squealing, and then suddenly none. It was unsettling and wholly natural.

Both of our cats were in the house and are therefore absolved. More likely the predator was a coyote or a fisher or an owl. We have lots of owls.

Unsettlement has been a recurring theme across a wide swath of public and private life lately. This is not all bad. Off and on this year I have been reading Nassim Nicholas Taleb's book *Antifragility*, and based on my lightweight understanding, living through unsettled times prepares us to live through unsettled times, so wow, I guess we've all been getting a lot of practice running in a circle on the same rug.

There is some relation between antifragility and hormesis, in which a small amount of a toxin or stressor strengthens us against same. A lot of your antifragile hormesis fanatics lift weights for just this reason. I myself have dabbled. My back felt stronger, but my unsettlement was not cured. I will get some bigger bricks.

If you are the critter who became dinner out there in the snowy woods, you are uninterested in my thoughts on hormesis. If this past pandemic year has kicked the slats out of your family, your job, your heart—you don't need some typist rattling on about fragility. I thought of that when I typed the words "This is not all bad." Among the chief reveals over the course of the recent past has been light regard for the fragile among us.

With deference in place, I continue to study up on antifragility. In part to validate my own amateur theories and in part to see if I can glean anything that will make me more a help and less a load for myself and others. By way of asterisk, let me say "study up" translates to "read five pages and get some sleep." It's usually late by the time I crack the book, which is as thick as the print is small. And Taleb sometimes writes as if he thinks I'm smarter than I am. Go figure.

Early this winter I went to fetch firewood and found myself stalled between the house and the barn, studying a series of oddly repetitive patterns in the snow. On closer examination they proved to be composed of small bootprints, many of which were interconnected by arcing sweeps and swoops traced through the flakes. Then I remembered. Earlier that day I looked out my window in the little room over the garage to see my daughter, twirling through the yard, reenacting the intricate dances of her beloved K-Pop.

I want to be antifragile. I also wish to never discount the beauty of fragility as it relates to the ephemeral and how it might lift our hearts, in this case through the remnant choreography of a child dancing in the great wide open.

Happy Days Painting

IN A CORNER OF MY OFFICE there hangs a framed poster of a young boy walking beside his dog on a sunlit dirt path. The boy has a cane pole in one hand and a mess of panfish dangling from the other. The lower left-hand corner of the poster is stamped with a blue badge emblazoned "U.S. ROYAL TIRES."

I've always assumed this poster came into the family via my father, a little boy who grew up in a river town and snagged his share of sunfish, but I realize just now I've never asked, and it could also have arrived via my mother, as they are both from Eau Claire, Wisconsin, longtime home of a giant Uniroyal tire plant affiliated with U.S. Royal. When Michelin acquired Uniroyal in 1990 and shuttered the plant in 1991, my future father-in-law was among those knocked out of a job.

The poster hung in our farmhouse throughout my childhood. On winter mornings I would lie abed staring at it and feel the sun filtering through those leaves, the warm dirt on my feet, the weight of the fish dangling from one hand. "Happy Days," says the title inscribed at the base of the poster beside a stylized bobber, and come summer I lived those happy days.

Fast forward 30-40 years. I'm up late writing in my little office over the garage. Making one more cup of coffee. Waiting for the water to boil and studying that poster as I have for nearly all my life. My eye falls on the signature of the artist who painted the original scene the poster reproduces: "Clair V. Fry." It occurs to me that I have never searched out that name on the internet. Probably because I've been looking at it since before computers.

The internet search led me to a website curated by Clair Fry's grandson, Jamey. I sent him an email. Jamey replied, saying his grandfather would be "grinning from ear to ear" if he knew his work was still being enjoyed, and that Clair was the "quintessential grandfather" and a role model loved by all. Jamey allowed as how the painting was likely based on a scene at his great-grandfather's trout farm north of Hudson, Wisconsin, and that the little boy was Jamey's uncle. After a few other stories and details, he closed by saying our exchange brought back a flood of fond memories.

Over time and with recent acceleration, my relationship with sentimentality and nostalgia has grown ever more ambivalent. On the downside, its mutations range from paralytic self-pity to heartless nationalism. When I stare into the image Clair V Fry left us, I recapture my child's wonder at the wide-open, unblemished possibility of a summer's day. And then, nibbling around the edges of the image, my adult's tempered expectations, the subliminal understanding that the painted sunshine may not be sufficient, that fond memories may ameliorate the present but cannot barricade against it.

As always, there is the temptation to stick a ribbon on the preceding paragraphs, to go all homily and "what-have-we-learned," when in fact the answer is ever-evolving, and the main force of fond memories and the totems that evoke them perhaps lies in the fact that they may not overcome present darkness but are stored, salted, and accessible in spite of it.

THE CARDINAL

THE CARDINAL APPEARED in the winter-stripped bush outside our window this morning with all the subtlety of a Christmas ornament left hanging after the needles drop. Those scarlet feathers are an invigorating sight any time of the year but perhaps especially in this the season of who-knows-what-season featuring a landscape of bleak browns and deteriorating whites.

I was happy to see him.

A cardinal is magical realism on the wing. You know beneath those feathers it's just another bird, and a fairly common one at that, but you also can't quite believe your luck when all that crimson flares up right outside your window. It opens you to the possibility of conjury. As he flew away I dubbed him a talisman of spring even though I know full well he's non-migratory.

You go from marveling at the cardinal to realizing you forgot to schedule the mortgage payment to tripping over a pair of shoes on your way to the computer to thinking now that I'm down here I can see I really oughta vacuum and how long has that thing been under the chair and did it just move, and before you know it, your to-do list has expanded rather than shrunk, and what you'd really like here in the terrestrial fact-based world is two cookies and a nap.

That little play-by-play is reflective of reality, which has never been my residence of choice but is also a reminder that lately I have been trending morose and self-dramatic when in fact in comparison to so much of the world my life is chocolate-dipped strawberries and a full-time sunshine fountain, and I might oughta lighten up.

To that end I have sketched out preliminary notes toward a treatise contending that the concepts of counterbalance and contrast may count among our most undervalued blessings. If everything went our way all the time, we might come to think we somehow deserved it and in the process blunt our ability to catch a buzz off life's intermittent daisies. Exhibit A: We undervalue dry socks until we have wet socks. Exhibit B: Four good tires never really register until you're searching for the jack and spare. Exhibit C: The exclamatory vision of a cardinal exponentially enhanced thanks to all the monochrome.

Two days have passed since I wrote the preceding paragraphs. Diversions, you know: vacuuming, payments due, naps, cookies, and whatnot. Meanwhile, the cardinal keeps popping up around the place. I saw him once while feeding the chickens and again while doing some yard work. And yet again as I walked to my little office above the garage where I spied him aground, scratching in the leaves. I had a word with him. Warned him all this ubiquity threatened to dilute his talismanic mystique. *Son*, he replied. *Look at these feathers. Should these babies ever lose their mystique, that dilution is due to you being a drip, not me.*

I nodded and resolved to henceforth walk in wonder.

Pruning Antlers

It might be spring or not, so we pruned the plum and apple trees. It was good to be in the sun. "We" was my wife and me, and based on our schedule of late, this counted as a date. At one point we stood there and held hands while the snow melted. It felt a little like high school, I'm happy to say.

The day prior, I went for a walk in the woods with my neighbor. We were hunting sheds while en route to look at some adjacent real estate.

"Sheds" in this case refers to shed antlers. I find them more exciting when attached to the deer, but over time shed hunting has become a most popular pursuit, and in fact there are dogs trained to hone in on horns. Before you click your corrective pen, I said "horns" on purpose and used "antlers" earlier only as a courtesy. When you come from where I come from, we know very well deer don't have horns, but we also carry an inherent suspicion of syllables. If you went to rhapsodizing on antlers, we just figured you were from out of town on a guided hunt and probably didn't even make your own sandwich. Or drag your own deer. Or wear your blaze orange hoodie all year 'round and thus the sad lack of ketchup, fry oil, and baler grease camo accents.

To this day I still prefer to declare a deer has big horns—there is blunt joy in twinning the unadorned words, whereas "big antlers" just sorta peters out while you're navigating that triconsonantal cluster—but now I have betrayed my own multisyllabic backsliding, for which I blame my Mom, as she taught me to read by the age of four and often left me unsupervised with the dictionary. I have furthermore been known to read philosophy books in my deer stand. Although this year I got back to my roots with some Louis L'Amour.

The neighbor and I returned from our hike empty-handed in all respects, having found neither horns nor antlers nor any kinda math that tallied up with us being able to afford the real estate as priced. That said, just this afternoon I received by direct deposit a royalty check of 38 cents, so I will plow it into a cryptocurrency ETF, say a prayer to the gods of compounding, and wait for the money to roll in. I shall pass the time researching tax brackets and looking up big words. Although why say dollars when you can say bucks.

Anyways. (As we say around these parts when we're not saying horns instead of antlers.) When I mentioned to my wife that the neighbor had called and asked to go on walkabout, she said, "When's the last time you went for a walk with your *wife?*" and now you know why I was out there pruning fruit trees and holding hands.

ROYAL'S LUCK

LAST WEEK MY DAD CALLED with good news about his neighbor Royal. Royal is not his real name, but that is the name we will use today. Royal is one of those folks whose last name you'd recognize if you were from where I'm from. Big family, been around the township for generations.

Royal's daughter and I went to school together from kindergarten through graduation. Royal served on the school board, and I remember him sitting behind me when I delivered the graduation speech, very likely rolling his eyes and thinking about his corn. Over the years Royal raised, harvested, and trucked enough corn to make Iowa jealous. He and his wife Kate (or so we'll call her today) even painted their LP tank to look like a giant corn cob. I always loved seeing that big cob, because it was comical and good-humored, and it meant I was getting close to home.

Some years back, Kate and Royal moved in just around the corner from my folks' farm and—accompanied by their loyal Australian shepherd dog Scoutie—became regulars at our informal Sunday evening get-togethers. Royal usually sits at the far end of the table, his ever-present ball cap emblazoned with the military outfit he served with as a younger man.

Kate died over a year ago, and Royal's in his 80s now. Most mornings he loads up Scoutie and goes to a little café in town and has pancakes for breakfast. As Dad told it to me, last week when Royal approached the register to pay his check, the cashier waved him off, explaining that someone had already picked up his tab. Royal turned and saw two men he didn't recognize. "Thank you for your service," they said.

Royal thanked them, climbed into his pickup truck, and headed over to the gas station, where he topped off the tank. When he returned to his truck after paying, he found a crumpled dollar bill on the ground beside the driver's side door. He picked it up and looked around, but there was no one in sight. So he went back into the gas station and bought a dollar scratch-off.

Back in the truck, he did his scratching. And won five bucks. So again he went into the gas station, this time buying a five-dollar scratch-off. Then he drove home, waiting to scratch the ticket until he was back in the house.

Whereupon he won fifty bucks.

That's all. That's the story. Not a life-changer, but what a sweet little run of luck. From free pancakes to half a C-note, all in the space of a morning.

I asked Dad to needle Royal a little, let him know I'd read an article once about how so many of these megamillion winner folk go off the deep end. Blow it all or die young.

Tell Royal I said not to let it go to his head, I told Dad. And I was smiling when I said it because I've known Royal enough to pretty much guess exactly what he'd say in reply: "Well it's too late for me to die young."

On occasion I am told I am getting too big for my literary britches. That I oughta dial it down. Simplify. I'm not so sure, because words are a tasty hoot, and no one's getting hurt. But you bet sometimes it's best to simply tell the story, and so there you have Royal's story as it was told to me.

Good luck.

BLACK DOG

LATELY I HAVE BEEN SPENDING a little more time than I'd prefer walking the black dog. Not even walking, really. More like we eye each other from opposite corners of the room, both thinking: "Oh. You again."

I am rich in reading but poor in remembering. This leads to knowing a little about a lot, but not a lot about any one thing. I do a lot of nodding in recognition but very little in-depth explaining unless the source materials are at hand. Keep that in mind when I declare the term "black dog" was coined as a euphemism for depression by the poet Horace, is cited in medieval literature, and was perhaps most famously invoked by Winston Churchill.

In my distant past I worked on a mental health unit. I sat in on group therapy sessions, I answered the suicide hotline, I wrote up heartbreaking nurse's notes. As such, I know the depths of my depression are but a dip in a teacup compared to what so many endure. I take the black dog seriously, but he doesn't have the run of the place, and he's never had me by the throat. But when he's around I don't take my eyes off him.

I also have blessed countermeasures at hand: My wife, a solid source of comfort and counsel; my children, who uplift and propel me in ways they may never know; and neighbors like Denny down the hill, who is my therapist without knowing so. Just two days ago I was motoring morosely along when I spotted him placing an envelope in his mailbox. I hit the brakes and lowered the pickup window.

"If that's a check for me, I'll just take it now," I said. "Save ya the stamp!"

"Ha!" he said. Then, waving the envelope with one hand while pointing at his house with the other, he said, "I'm mailing this so I can keep that!" There followed some goofball back-and-forth, and Denny wouldn't know it and doesn't need to hear it, but when I turned up the hill toward our farm I was lighter in my heart. This is no doubt tied to the fact that some of my current darkness is drawn from the general determination of a large portion of our population to cast each other as irredeemably idiotic. I have to guard against this myself and find talking to the neighbors helps.

I don't mean to suggest the black dog is easily brought to heel. I'm thinking right now of all the farmers we've lost to suicide. I hope openness about mental health continues to grow. We've come a long way since I was writing up those nurse's notes, but so much work remains.

The dog is dark, but today I got off light. After a cold gray morning, the sun busted out and illuminated the tiniest slice of green peeking from a bud on a branch outside my window. It was a work of natural art, a metaphor, a reason to wait around and see what comes next.

I hope you can feel the sun. And if the black dog is blocking it, you need not face the darkness alone.

Laundry Line

Comes that first day when you walk into the wind and it is not your adversary. There is no need to brace, to tense your cheeks against the chill, to yank the zipper pull chin-ward, to tug the cap tighter to your skull. Today is the first day following winter when finally the air is warm enough that you can just wade in without so much as a windbreaker. No need to dip your toe or lead with a scarved snoot. You can brave the atmosphere without hugging yourself.

It'll be a while yet before the wrens nest, and the buds have just begun to split, and the ten-day forecast is a deteriorating disappointment skewing toward hoodies and sweaters and umbrellas, but today for the first time since sometime last autumn you could just step through the door without pausing to apply an extra layer, and this to those of us emerging from the season of bundling is an exquisite freedom.

When I was a kid at grade school recess we always marveled at how warm ten degrees above zero felt after January as opposed to before January. The body adjusts, yes, but even more so the mind. And if ten above feels warm in the new year, imagine how tropic the first gnat hatch, or the sound of flies buzzing at the screen.

At lunchtime I took a load of laundry to the deck and hung it, this too a first for the year. The wind was kicking up now, testing the clothespins, but rather than rushing like an icy rapids, it flowed like soft surf. With the exception of a single extended subzero stretch where I had to run a heavy-duty extension cord into the basement to keep the pipes from solidifying, we got off relatively lightly this winter. But the contrast is sufficient, and it's nice to be pleased by the weather. To feel it like a gift rather than a chore. At this point in my life, the turn in temperature is hardly a fresh experience, and yet it feels so, and if rediscovery feels like discovery, then you just go ahead and float on it.

We know better than to go all tank tops and flip-flops. There is still a mixed stack of split oak and box elder beside the woodstove, and a scuttle of kindling. Tonight there is rain inbound. Already I have heard some thunder. This is fine, because the grass will spring up and the chickens will switch to grazing mode, and we'll get that magical week where the lawn looks full and green but the mower can stay stowed. In fact, if the temperatures follow their predicted course, that grass will stay close to ground for an extra week.

For now we ignore the fact that the air conditioner will need to be lugged upstairs and stuck in the window. That there will be days so thick with heat we will retreat to our cubes of manufactured frigidity and strategically placed fans.

I can appreciate the clear-glass purity of twenty below. Likewise I don't mind heat and humidity because I remember twenty below. But there is no sweet spot like that first day when the weather is not too cold, not too hot, but dead-on dialed-in Goldilocks perfect. When the air is fine and laundry luffs on the line.

SUNK COST

YESTERDAY MY FITNESS ROUTINE included ripping and dragging cattle panels out of the underbrush in a cold rain. There is a logger coming to trim the trees I let grow too big too long too close to our pole barn. If I don't pull the panels they'll be crushed. And if I cut those trees down myself, the pole barn will be crushed.

So there I was, damp, muddy, and festooned with wet burdock burrs, hacking and yanking away. There was buckthorn to be bushwhacked and popple to be chain-sawed before I could even approach the panels. Then I had to cut the triple-twist wiring tying the panels to the posts, three twists per post. I twisted all that wire myself way back when, and I am sad to say I did a fine job.

Many of the panels were braided with grapevine, some of which had grown thick as a garden hose. For those I used a lopper. Finally the bases of the panels were knitted to the earth by many year's worth of weeds and vines and the earth itself, into which the panels had sunk. This is where the yanking came in.

If I never become a billionaire, I'm gonna blame these cattle panels. They represent what your corporate finance folks call a "sunk cost"— money that has already been spent and cannot be recovered. Although some of those panels and posts came with the farm and were thus "repurposed," the majority of them were purchased fresh at the farm store or at auction. Perhaps I will one day recoup a portion of those funds through an auction of my own, but the bulk of the sunk cost got sank through the most irretrievable currency of all: Time.

I had pigs back then. Figured I'd expand into beef. Or beefers, as my people say. I had a whole plan about how I'd fence the old barnyard with fresh barbwire, then construct a long chute from the barnyard out past the pole barn where it would open into the main pasture.

I worked at it for weeks. Drafted my buddy Mills. We got the job done. But I never got the beefers.

Life happened, a lot of it on the road. Selling books, selling stories. In time I even had to let the pigs go. In the big picture this is as it should have been, because as someone raised on a working farm I've always known I wasn't a farmer.

And yet as I pulled those panels I felt a twinge of regret. Over time I had developed this little routine in which I joked about raising "theoretical" beef, which is the best kind of livestock for a typist such as I. And yet I still harbored a thread of hope that I might one day look out back and see the real thing, grazing hillside.

All this time the weeds and burdock and grapevine never stopped working. The trees I should have been trimming kept reaching outward and ever nearer the pole barn. Disasters aside, nature wins through patience.

The cattle panels are now stowed in the pole barn and recategorized as part of my retirement portfolio. Some investment hotshots are into cattle futures; I'm into *cattle panel* futures. When the time is right, I'll cash out. Should I cash out first, well, into the estate sale they go. La-di-da. Much of life is built on sunk cost; I'll count it a blessing to break even.

April Snowflake

Few snowflakes are crueler than the April snowflake. As it flittered past the teensy leaves of the apple tree this morning, it whispered, "Yah, not so fast there."

I write this in a week of uncertainty, as if certainty were ever anything but a blind privilege. Snow in April is the least of it. I find myself grateful for the trash needing taking out, the chicken coop needing moved, the dirt-kicking simplicity of shooting the breeze with a logger, which I did earlier this week. I can hear his chainsaw now. He knocks off earlier than I do, but if I did what he does I would tip over by noon. When I introduced myself, I broke the ice by telling him I was apprenticed to and related to loggers but—and then I showed him my hands—was no longer in the business.

This got a big laugh, and gave us a place to start.

I am ever hopeful about the human condition, and equally despairing. Who knows the headlines surrounding this text right now. They flip over like arrival and departure times in a helter-skelter subway terminal. This, I think, is why we resent that April snowflake. It was sunny, it was warm, and wham, the weather turned. Doesn't matter if we saw it coming; we're still not happy it's here.

I have lately made it my assignment to wrench my introverted hinder out of the writing chair and make conversation with the neighbors, including a few I've not met before. This is no sacrifice but it is unnatural, as my favorite place in the world is in a tiny room all alone, and when it comes to basic social skills, I ramble like a flat-footed clogger on a bender minus any sense of rhythm. I avoid human contact for days on end, then I encounter a fellow person and the words babble forth in a river of jabber. More than once I have apologized for this, but probably not often enough. I often see a look of light bewilderment in my conversation partner's eyes, reflecting not so much a desire to escape as amazement at the amount of oxygen I'm burning in a straight line.

But eventually I hear myself and shut up. And then the neighbor talks. And then an hour is gone, and we do the mossy old joke about not solving the world's problems, but in fact we have made incremental progress on one of the world's problems, because the undercurrent here is my neighbors and I do not see all things in this world the same, but here we are talking, not posting. And if we talk long enough—if we persist through my babble—we brush up against these things. The logger and I covered some ground in this regard. Neither yielded, but we still wave at each other of a morning and can't help but perceive of each other as human.

The flake I spotted today melted as soon as it hit the ground. No accumulation is predicted. But it was the emotional equivalent of a wet burdock burr down my boot. In moments like these, one must get a grip and focus on the positives. I know that's what I'm reaching for here today. Not ten feet from where that snowflake melted a tulip is rising. It's not a metaphor, it's a tulip. We want to hope. Even as we brace for what may come. For those snowflakes in May.

Phone Rescue

Last week i received a mysterious call from a friend. His voice was animated but distant, as if he was hollering from inside a barrel, possibly while rolling around in the back of a truck.

"MIKE?"

"MIKE?"

"CAN YOU HEAR ME?"

I kept saying his name and saying I could hear him, but he clearly couldn't hear me.

There followed silence and what sounded like more clunking.

Then I heard his voice again, still muffled and as if from a distance. Now he was yelling, "Hey Siri! Hey Siri! Hey Siri!"

"I can hear you," I said. "Can you hear me?"

"Hey Siri!"

Then we disconnected.

I'm generally slow to alarm, but I was immediately uneasy. I knew this particular friend was on a three-day solo drive through a remote part of the West. He is also a tech whiz with a calm demeanor. Not the sort of fellow to go around helplessly yelling at his handset. I wondered if he was lying injured some distance from his phone. Or if he had been abducted.

I dialed him twice, and both calls went straight to voice mail. So I sent him two texts and an email, pasting the same message into each in the hopes one might get through: *got phone call from you then disconnected and heard you talking to Siri just checking yr OK*

Just then I got a text from an unfamiliar number: *Yo! This is me.* (He used his name—I won't.)

Ah, good, I texted with relief.

He replied: *Do you still have my car app?*

Well over a year ago I borrowed his vehicle. It's one of those new ones that comes with its own app, and I had downloaded it to my phone. I checked, and sure enough, buried several screens deep beside the Yatzy, there it was.

I confirmed, and he texted back: *can you log in and unlock my car?*

And so it was, from a distance of 2,102 miles and three time zones, I tapped my phone, and shortly thereafter received a text from what was now obviously a phone he'd borrowed from a stranger: *he's in.*

Dude, I texted back to his recovered phone, *I feel like we just landed on Mars.*

It's a shining moment in human progress, he replied. Then, *Holy cow that was a clusterREDACTED. Car key, phone, and Apple Watch, all locked in the car.*

He thanked me then, and we both prepared to go about our day. But then I got to thinking...and texted him again: *Wait a minute...WERE YOU YELLING AT SIRI THROUGH THE WINDOW!?!?*

LIKE A MAD MAN, he replied.

As of this writing he is safely back home, but we have yet to speak in person. I have exceptionally high hopes for the reenactment.

STRAW BALES

AT NOON MY WIFE INVITED ME to join her on a trip to get some straw bales from our farmer neighbor Jerry. I told her I was too busy then relented because busy is a silly word in the face of a ride down a country road with your steady when the blossoms are out and you will never live this day again.

That escalated quickly.

Off we went then, my wife at the wheel, a sight that tickles some of the old-timers around here who love to needle me about not being able to drive myself. I like to think I'm modeling some version of the modern emancipated male. In fact she just got to the truck first.

Anneliese knows how to throw a hay bale, having grown up throwing them by the thousands, as did I. And if you did too, then you know straw bales are as wiffle balls are to baseballs. Same size, much lighter, and you can toss them in ways you could never toss a bale of clover, timothy, or alfalfa.

It was good to be in the haymow together, Jerry the neighbor pointing out the bale pile he wanted us to take from, Anneliese tossing them down, me packing them in the truck, the upper story of the barn a muffled cavern cut with light slanting through gaps in the siding. They say scents are evocative, but the vision of a sunbeam full of floating chaff will put a swirl in your spirit. You inhabit your younger self, kneeing the bales into place, spin-tossing them so they land cut-side up or twine-side up, depending on the fit. Memory and muscle memory, all sync'd up.

We took 15 bales total. Compared to the old days, that's not even worth greasing the baler. But the old days are just that. We aren't tucking our cows in for the winter, we're lining the chicken coop and mulching the garden.

When it came time to settle up there was trouble, one of those reverse skirmishes in which Jerry refused to let us pay the full price he'd quoted on the phone ("I think you're doing your math wrong," he said, knowing full well we weren't), and Anneliese (who was running the wallet as well as the pickup) insisted on nothing less and dug out the cash. Usually the phrase "money changed hands" indicates a one-way transaction. In this case the bills went back and forth like the two of them were playing a passive-aggressive game of Go Fish.

In the end, the ritual culminated in us accepting the discount and Jerry accepting a dozen fresh eggs. Both parties called it square. We shot the breeze a while, caught up, and then made our way home, hearts lifted as they always are when human interaction leaves you with hope for humans.

Anneliese went off to an appointment, and I returned to my desk, where busy always waits, so you might as well just hop in the truck and go.

Electricity

THE LOCAL ELECTRIC COOPERATIVE did us a big favor this week, removing the overhead lines that run from our house down through a steep wooded ravine and replacing them with buried cables. I doubt this was the biggest project of their year, but it was big to us, and we sure appreciate it.

I don't know what the cooperative records would show, but on average over the fourteen years we've lived here it seems the power has gone out a couple times each of those years, and more often than not the trouble can be traced to the lines running that ravine. A branch separates from a storm-whipped tree, and off go the lights.

When you plug in the toaster at our house, you are tapping the terminal end of the line, juice-wise. There are no other homes hooked in beyond ours. This meant whenever the power did go out, we had to call, because it could be just us. I always feel bad calling because I assume the crews are already being bombarded, and we know they'll get to us as soon as they can, but if it's just us in the dark, how will they know?

Just now as I'm writing this I realize it's no longer 1969, and the co-op probably knows the power is off before we touch the phone.

Last year I decided it was time to buy a generator in case one of these outages lasted longer than usual. (You will note it took me over a decade to draw this conclusion—draw your own conclusions.) There was, as the saying goes, "some assembly required." I strategically situated the box in the garage so I'd have to look at it every time I got in the van and be reminded to conduct said assembly.

Which is to say when the power went out three months later I knew exactly where to find the box and start assembling like sixty because there was about an hour of daylight left before I'd be working with a flashlight in my teeth.

At the very cusp of dusk I tightened the last nut, topped the tank, and yanked the starter cord. The generator came to life, and my daughter—who had been handing me wrenches—tapped me excitedly on the shoulder. "Neat, right?" I said, as usual unduly proud of the simplest mechanic achievement. Then I noticed she was pointing toward the house, which was glowing with incandescent light. The power was back on. She giggled at my impeccable timing, and I joined her.

With the new wires tucked safely into the dirt, we shouldn't need that generator as often as anticipated. And that's just fine. My wife and I stopped down to thank the crew and tell them we appreciated what they were doing. "*We* appreciate it," said one of the hard hats, chuckling and nodding toward the ravine they'd all come to know all too well over the years, usually during the most inclement of conditions. "Every time your address popped up, we knew what we were in for." Now everyone chuckled and nodded, and for just a moment in this tangled world two perspectives converged, and if I'm making a big deal out of a little deal, I feel the same when I flip a switch and light pours forth.

SENTIMENTALITY

SENTIMENTALITY IS MY CHIEF AFFLICTION.

I am trying to remedy that.

I have no interest in hardening my heart, although there are plenty of days I think life would be easier were my cardiac componentry clad in cast iron. Rather, I am trying to find a way to honor the past without drowning in it. Or fashioning it into something it never was. Or sit bogged in it as the present whooshes over me.

This all sounds self-dramatic, which is why I am prone to sentimentality in the first place. It is by dictionary definition excessive. It is also the perfect form of excess for introverts. The drama trends toward misty-eyed quietude and yearning and staring out windows.

My childhood was by any definition idyllic. Raised by parents who loved me, I never went to bed hungry. I spent my days exploring the surrounding woods, reading books on a screen porch filled with birdsong, and doing just enough farm chores to respect physical labor.

I knew early I wasn't cut out to be a farmer, but I loved that farm. You could stand me on any acre and I'd have a story. I came to feel the land, the arrangement of the buildings, even the sound of the place as an integral part of me. Well into my thirties I stewed over how I might keep it in the family should no other member be interested or able. I stood in the echoey stairwell I used to climb in my Winnie the Pooh pajamas and couldn't imagine displacing this family history with another family's history.

At some point things began to change. The land surrounding our farm was reconfigured. Small meadows became big fields. Woodlots were replaced by irrigation circles. One day I drove home and just after crossing the Beaver Creek culverts, I realized I could see clear across all the open country to the family back forty, which had always been cozily hidden behind treelines.

Somewhere in that moment, something loosened. I wasn't happy about what I saw, but I also realized I had been freed from the imaginary (and self-aggrandizing) responsibility of preservation predicated by memory. That my energies were better focused elsewhere.

Last Sunday I walked the home place with my parents. Change—both on the farm and surrounding properties—has continued apace. There are also many tangible ties to the past still in evidence: The squat shed I remember playing in as a child, when it was still stocked with the plumbing supplies of the previous owner; the old pole barn that was the new pole barn when the crew put it up during a stretch of weather so hot Dad loaded everyone up for a rare afternoon trip to the local swimming hole; the original standalone milk house where the cans were kept cool in a water bath.

Driving away from the farm afterward, I was pleased to find the pleasure of those memories outweighed any desire to preserve the place they sprang from. I was happy to revisit them but no longer compelled to physically enshrine them. Slowly my sentimentality has been leavened with sensibility.

Down here on our place we just had a logger clear-cut a 20-acre patch of woods, and I was dreading the sound of his saw. But he's finished now, and last night I stepped out on the crest of the hill and saw not a gaping hole but a whole new vista. The memories are set, the future awaits.

Michael Perry

FIRE CIRCLE

WE LIT A FIRE and sat around it, taking our turns in the smoke and taking our turns at the stories.

It doesn't get much more old-fashioned than that. Clear back to the caves.

We were four friends, largely separated over the past year. Nothing dramatic had come between us, nothing amounting to a speck of sacrifice in the big picture, just current events, occupations, and geography. And a wee pandemic. Now we had a chance to be in the same place at the same time.

One of us arrived by Tesla, one by rental car, one by beat-up pickup truck, and one by foot, as he owns the place. Earlier I did spot him tooling around in a UTV, which he admits he deploys more in the name of regional credibility than utility. He is an artist living amongst hunters and farmers. His credibility is not all artifice; last year he got a dandy big buck deer. Also let's not get carried away: We are surrounded by working farms, but there are also a pharmacist, a chiropractor, at least two government employees, and possibly a millionaire in the neighborhood so it's not like camo and barn boots are required to check the mail.

An aside: Does anyone still say "tooling around?" I learned that one from my dad and think it deserves a comeback.

The view before us was a horse pasture, property of the neighbors. One of those cleanly kept, neatly fenced expanses circumscribed by electrified white tape. The horses looked civilized and grand, grazing shoulder to shoulder. (I wanted to write "pastern to pastern" but had to look up "pastern" in the dictionary, a sure sign I was out of my league and overreaching for a "pasture/pastern" echo.) The grass and surrounding wooded hillsides were spring green, which is to say one color in multitudinous versions, broken across the valley by a single blot of maroon.

"That's a maple, right?" asked the musician, pointing out the blot.

"Yep," I said. "I once wrote of their color as a 'rubrous blush.'"

"Yah, well my Dad calls it 'matchstick red.'"

"I'd say go with your dad on that one."

And so it went, a meandering conversation punctuated by friendly jabs, the sort you earn over time and serve with a smile. The artist lately fancies himself a birder. When a hawk flew over and he nonchalantly remarked, "Red-tail," I facetiously congratulated him on identifying one of the tough ones. Next up, a robin.

The day was cool and gray with a light bluster of wind, the sort you get when intermittent rains are due. We didn't want to get wet, but on behalf of our real farmer neighbors with their parched, unsprouted rows (my own oats had poked out an inch and then stalled), we wanted the rain.

It misted just enough that we moved inside the garage, but it wasn't until we were all gone our separate ways that the real rain came. It fell steadily overnight. Come morning the oats had jumped a half inch and the air smelled of renewal.

DUNKIN' DOZER

SPECTACLE TAKES MANY FORMS, and this week in our neighborhood it was a very large bulldozer stuck in the mud.

First, let us pause in respectful consideration of the dozer operator: We are not gathered to mock him. Word on the street (rural road) has it this was his very first day at the controls, and he had been at the job less than an hour. Some things can only be learned through experience, and it is my fervent hope that he will be allowed a second chance. Were I fired the first time I broke that hay swather in Wyoming I might still be hitchhiking home.

Our focus today is not on the individual, but rather on the broader human tendency to engage in genial celebration of another's misfortune as long as no one got hurt. Or at least not badly hurt. Barked knuckles and head knocks can be hilarious. A buried bulldozer is free entertainment, simple as that.

I was returning from an errand in town when I spotted the giant implement sunken and askew in the field neighboring our property. Any farm kid sent to till springtime fields is familiar with the parting admonition: "Don't get stuck!" Stuck means time lost. Stuck means trudging off to your boss. At the sight of that dozer, my mouth circled into an involuntary "ohhh...."

I spied my neighbor Denny gawking from his yard and pulled directly into his driveway so we could review the situation. He told me about the novice operator, and how he had seen the whole thing happen, and how it had sunk another several inches since.

A favorite family saying in these circumstances is, "Wha'jou DO?" For example, when my younger brother Jed was using my older brother John's excavator and the hydraulics failed in such a manner as to convert the machine into a very expensive monument, rather than rage or wring his hands, John just looked at Jed, poked out his lips, and said, "Wha'jou DO?"

Try it sometime, whether you just shucked the transmission on your log skidder or dropped a dish in the kitchen. It's a terrific defuser and tends to impose perspective: In the course of human events, what is a shattered pickle tray or marooned bulldozer? "Wha'jou DO?" I said, and Denny and I giggled without malice.

By the time the owner trailered in an excavator to extricate the dozer, our little crowd had grown. We were joined by my teenaged daughter, Denny's wife Linda, our neighbor Marty from one side of the road, and our neighbor Ginny from the other. My daughter hugged Ginny and Linda for the first time since the pandemic, and we all engaged in catch-up, banter, and light gossip. When they began tugging at that dozer, we speculated and commentated, making fun of ourselves for gawking even as we gawked. At some point I realized we were all standing there not checking our phones.

The excavator dragged the dozer to solid ground and yet we remained, visiting about this and that and the new neighbors moving in over there off the dead end road and how the corn was or wasn't coming along and eventually someone said, "Well, I s'pose," and we made our separate ways, and I'm sorry that man got stuck, but I sure do appreciate the get-together he precipitated.

THE WAVE

A CITY READER submits the following correspondence regarding rural driving etiquette:

> One of the country practices that I'm still trying to figure out is how and when or if to acknowledge the driver in the vehicle that passes us going the other way. I've noticed that some oncoming drivers will acknowledge us or our car with a wave or lifting one finger or two fingers off the steering wheel. Some drivers don't do that. Because I like receiving that friendly acknowledgement I have started doing that when I'm the driver.
>
> Even though I don't live in the country, is it acceptable—or at least not an affront to the other driver— for me to wave or raise one or two fingers? Assuming that it is acceptable, should I acknowledge every car we pass? If not every car how do I know or decide which one(s) to acknowledge? When an oncoming driver waves/acknowledges first should I respond in kind?

Last question first: Yes. If someone waves at you, wave back. An unacknowledged wave sows the seeds of social distrust. Also, if like me you are a rolling ball of latent guilt and look up to see someone waving just as you meet and before you can wave back, you will spend the next three miles fighting the urge to whip a U-ey, chase them down, and flail the air like you're trying to attract the attention of a Coast Guard chopper—all so they don't think you're "a stuck-up."

Should you wave at every car you pass? On a country road, yes. You are excused once you hit the highway, a roundabout, or oncoming traffic averages more than two vehicles per minute. Tractors? You always wave at tractors.

My daughters (possibly while rolling their eyes) will tell you I wave at every person we meet between our farm and their school drop-off. There is a reason for this. I had begun to notice that even the country drivers are in a rush or crossing the centerline while checking their meme stocks or scrolling their favorite anger-feed. For quite a while I gave up on waving. Then one morning as I drove them to school, my daughters were discussing differences and yard signs, and I decided it was time to bring back the wave. If it makes me look like a rube, so be it. If I am ignored, fine. But more often than not I get a wave back. It is my naïve hope that what we are doing here is acknowledging each other as humans.

And so we come to the wave itself. Mainly, be subtle. Don't go at it like you're scrubbing the windshield, lest they think you need 911 or a wasp popped out of your defroster. I go with the single index finger raised lazily from the steering wheel, two fingers if I'm feeling heartier. You can raise your whole hand if you wish, or do the seed-corn-cap brim-brush salute, but depending on traffic that gets to be a lot of work. We familiar knuckleheads sometimes like to greet each other with aggressive finger-pointing. To the untrained eye this can appear accusatory; in fact it's jocose sign language for, "Ha-Ha! We are playing hooky!"

If you meet my Dad in his beat-up wood hauler, he will flash a "V for Victory" sign, although I assume everyone just figures it's a peace sign, and in truth he is far more a peace guy than a victory guy. And in that very spirit may we forever wave.

Van Again

By the time you read this I hope to have been up to the Bayfield area in my tour van to tell some stories in a tent, specifically the Lake Superior Big Top Chautauqua, which is perched high atop a hill overlooking Lake Superior and the Apostle Islands, a collection of jade dollops in the freshwater blue.

The folks who run the tent are finding their way back into things, as are we all. I have referred to the past year as a time of great clarification, take that as you will. I'm above all just happy to be once again packing up the van and hitting the road. I have been known to yammer on about how I am a loner and lover of solitude, and by and large it is so, but sometimes when I'm surrounded by good and gregarious folk, I just can't help but enjoy myself. We've all done our best with what they call "connectivity," but happy laughter and freewheeling chatter lose something in electronic translation. Some sounds you need to *feel*.

I did so little road time last year I never took the snow tires off the tour van. I like to say tour van, as it implies a certain professional flash, never mind that it's a 2002 Toyota with a duct-taped license plate, two hubcaps, and four out of five doors that work. Regarding that fifth door, it's all about economics related to the cost of repair in order to move from 80% access to 100% access. I use a variation on the same formula to calculate snow tire wear versus remounting costs. In this case I'll be dropping the van off with our "guy" so he can switch out the tires but leave that stuck door be. He understands, or he wouldn't be working on vans like mine. Last year I was motoring sedately through one of the most dangerous traffic spots known to man—a high school parking lot just as the kids were turned loose—when a young scholar backed smack into my van, and despite the resounding crunch, I didn't even flinch. Among the joys of driving junk is blithe equanimity regarding fender benders.

We just picked up another used van as the price was right, and considering the current market for "previously loved" vehicles and the state and cumulative mileage of the tour van and another pending teenaged driver, it is good to hold some economical transport in reserve. The tailgate on this "new" van opens and closes by itself, which has led to me doing a lot of dodging and ducking. Also it was very well cared for by the previous owner, and it turns out we need only *change* the oil as opposed to *feed* it oil.

This was not intended to be an automotive report, but here we are. I hope you have been allowed some fresh air and sunlight of late, and the good company of good humans. Off we go.

HEAD BUTT

FIRST THING I DID THIS MORNING was dive into a spruce tree while trying to catch a chicken.

What I would tell you is: don't do that.

It's a deceptive tree, the spruce. Its boughs drape downward in a graceful sweep. The word *boughs* itself—with the "gh" dissipating into thin air—conjures softness and breeze. One imagines plunging in only to be lowered gently to the ground as if in the arms of mother.

Turns out there is *lumber* in there. Lumber of a sharp sort. I emerged with a red scrape traversing my pate from fore to aft.

I knew better, of course. Boughs notwithstanding, it is after all a *pine tree*. Needles, branches, bark, etc. But have you ever stepped out into the golden morn with your day all carefully planned and then wound up having to chase a chicken? Around and around? In the dew, gnats, and humidity? By the time she ducked beneath that spruce, I had worked myself into an antisocial and anaerobic state, which may have clouded my thinking.

It was one of those situations where you're grateful there were no witnesses. But then my first thought as I felt the sting of sweat seeping into my scored scalp was, *I'm gonna have to explain this all week long.*

I rarely mourn my departed hair. By the time it began falling out, I had other priorities. But there are two instances in which I dearly miss it. One is when I am seated beneath an air-conditioning vent. The other is when I pull a doofus move like head-butting a conifer. You fully-follicled folks can tattoo the score of *Cats* on your scalp, and no one will be the wiser. But let me forget to duck for the furnace duct or craniate an open cupboard door, and the whole world reads the story on my dome. I first realized this back in the freshly bald days when I gouged my head on a protruding roofing nail in my garage. Later that week two different people asked how I hurt myself. I was baffled until they pointed to my head, and I realized my clumsiness was inscribed for all to see.

I have a series of meetings this week. Relatively important meetings. Not involving state secrets or cryptocurrency regulation or modeling contracts, but meetings in which I hope to convey some minimal competence. And in at least a couple of cases, convey that competence to someone I've not met before.

I should probably explain the head wound right up front. Provide context. Although here just a few hours out I'm puzzling over exactly how one frames the phrase "I ran into a tree while chasing a chicken" in such a way that it instills trust, confidence, and investment. There is some irony in the fact that one of the meetings is related to intellectual property. It is possible the parties across the table will look at my head and doubt I possess any.

The Fire Hall

I ROLLED UP TO MY HOMETOWN last Friday to drop off some items for the fire department raffle. It was good to step inside the hall and smell the memories. If that sounds like a joke, it isn't. The scent was tires and canvas, all underlain with smoke. And stillness.

The stillness was always my favorite part. The stillness tells us things are good right now. Were I to choose my favorite meditation space, it would be in the middle of a fire hall between calls. Everything is set, prepped, and aligned. All in order, in anticipation of disorder.

Even as it implies there has been trouble before and will be trouble again, a well-ordered fire hall also implies a few of your fellow human beings have committed in advance to pitch in and fight it. Mitigate it. Show up when you call. This too sets a peaceful mood.

A handful of those humans were in the hall when I arrived with the raffle goods. Fourteen years have passed since I last served beside my neighbors on this department, so I didn't know everyone in attendance, but there were a couple with whom I have quite literally trusted my life. You see us shaking hands and goofing and leaning and yammering and the whole thing is underlain—there's that word again—with smoke and fire and death and blood and things you pray will never happen.

Tragedy is the bonding agent, but the memories we always find our way to are the goofy ones. We may revisit a rescue, but mainly we go straight to needling each other. Last Friday was no different, and my old friends delighted in telling the newcomers about the time I scorched a fire hose, the time they had to put out a fire in my thinning hair, and the time I left my radio unattended, which led to an elaborate practical joke. Rather than return my radio, they hid it. After I went home—still unaware I'd left the radio—a member of the department called me and, impersonating a local sheriff's deputy (the statute of limitations has long since expired on that one and frankly the deputy would have approved), informed me they had caught some kids broadcasting over my radio and could I meet them down at the village park so we could sort it all out.

When I arrived at the park, the firefighters who actually had my radio were waiting, but the joke took an unexpected and coincidental twist when—just as the pranksters were about to reveal themselves and return my radio—a pair of sheriff's deputies drove into the park to address an unrelated issue, at which point I excused myself, saying, "I gotta go talk to those deputies...they have my radio."

Decades old, this prank, and yet when we relived it for the new folks last Friday, we laughed as hard as if it were unfolding in real time. The lesson here for rookies is, just because you trust someone with your life doesn't mean you should trust them with your radio.

I was due at a meeting and couldn't stay long, but we did cover some ground. The fire hall is new since I left, so I've never hung my helmet there, but the scent aligns with my memory, and those goofball stories are solidly ours, and for this privilege of history I drove away thankful.

Fourth of July

I spent this Fourth of July outside the United States of America. Those in service to our military do it all the time. Also, sometimes our politicians, depending on who's inviting.

In my case our family was simply accepting the kindness of friends who offered us lodging.

Here we reside in a cacophonous nexus of sound: dogs barking often and at all hours, raucous two- and four-wheeler engine exhausts echoing off bricks and cobbles and up and down shoulder-scrapingly narrow streets, sparrows that sound like the ones back home and other birds that don't. The houses are built tightly together—fused, in fact—but the yards are walled. We are packed together in isolation, except for the sounds of conversations and celebrations, which rise, carry, and mingle. Sounds, and the aromatics of food. This morning I walked the streets early and at every other corner was treated to the scent of fresh-baked bread. It was the living definition of "wafting."

I do not speak the language of this place. I know some words, but vocabulary is not conversation. I make my best effort, communicating at the level of a slow-witted toddler. The hope is to convey sincerity and respect as opposed to presumption. It usually works out, and when it doesn't, the results are usually humorous. Once I asked for ice and got Oreos.

At midday on the Fourth I climbed to the roof and sat in the sun for a birds-eye view of our surroundings. The town is a dense conglomeration of stucco cubes arranged up and down mountain slopes and along a valley. The dogs were at it, as ever. From the house next door arose the sound of someone singing ABBA's "Dancing Queen" in a voice so off-key I found it a wonder equivalent to anything I'd ever heard in tune. To convey joy with an instrument so detuned is a marvel to be studied and respected.

The sky was blue and popcorned with clouds. Come late afternoon they would bank behind the mountain in a skulk, then breach to slide downslope and across the valley, draping gray veils of rain across the landscape. Most days the rains are brief. Come evening you can stroll the town square and leave your umbrella in the house.

Earlier I scanned the news from home. The country of my birth has been a blessing I do not take for granted. I honor those who preserve it in person, in truth, and in principle. But perched here on this foreign roof I was reminded again how time spent in a place with paving bricks older than our Declaration of Independence and monuments and buildings testament to events far preceding all but our native history renders certain stripes of bluster just that. To declare ourselves chosen is to unwittingly echo the chorus of every failed civilization preceding. Faith without works, etc., etc.

Fresh history or old history, all evidence suggests humans never learn; on the upside, they never give up. Back home, my flagpole is over 30 feet tall. Harrumph. But in a place where the birds sound different, it is good to hear new old songs. It's less about being number one than numbered among many. "I love it here," my daughter said after I'd climbed back down, "and it will be good to be back home."

Scanned

Once upon a time early in my fatherhood and before we all had cameras on our phones, my wife and daughter were traveling, and I was home alone in my office missing them. I had just purchased a nifty full-color flatbed scanner and had a working knowledge of email attachments, so I lifted the lid and scanned myself making a goofy dad-face.

So it was in the time of pioneers. We had to make do.

I rediscovered the scan this week while searching for some other image. In the old days I'd have been riffling through snapshots in a shoebox; in this case I was arrow-keying through a vast archive of digital images that have accumulated and cascaded down through a series of outdated and outmoded (and in one case, smoking) computers and Zip Disks and CD-Rs and standalone digital cameras and flip phones, right up to the business receipt I snapped with my phone three minutes ago. We are all archivists now. The scrapbooking will require an eternity.

During the scan, I failed to hold my pose, so my face and cranium are oval and elongated, as if a potato subsumed an eggplant. The result lands somewhere between cartoon and uncanny valley. My beard stubble and eyebrows are much, much darker compared to the frosty fringe I now sport, and even through the distortion there is a certain freshness around the edges of my eyes suggesting there have been some missed naps over the intervening sixteen years.

In part I blame the very child for whom I scanned my snoot. I loved her then and I love her now, but my face then and my face now stand testament to the ways parenting is not always picture perfect.

But above all, that scan calls into question whether I should have been entrusted with a child at all. Because I remember: Even as I leaned over to hold my face a half-inch above the glass, even as I punched the button, even as I made the goofball face, I remember thinking *what if this is dumb, well it is dumb, but what if it is dangerous* and yet resolutely holding my eyeballs wide open as a kajillion candlepowers pan-seared my retinas. It felt like self-propelled Lasik using a lightsaber taped to a Taser.

I staggered around for a while seeing nothing but the pulsing imprint of blinding illumination. It was like my eyeballs were locked inside a lava lamp.

After 30 years volunteering as a firefighter and medical first responder, I am the dad who sees death and injury lurking in everything from marshmallows to wading pools. My children were raised on safety speeches. And yet here I was self-welding my corneas. Some stories you save for decades before sharing them with the kids.

The kid in question is now 21 years old. I sent my scanner-selfie to her phone from my computer with a click. She texted a reply almost immediately: "Glad your sight came back. The thought was there, though." Then came the heart emoji, and with apologies to cringing ophthalmologists everywhere, I regret nothing.

Hummingbird Hostas

THE HUMMINGBIRDS have been hard at it amongst the hostas of late, and more power to them. Sunday morning as we brunched on the deck, they were all buzz and zip, doing their back-and-forth blossom business and providing entertainment to boot.

Brunch has always been an awkward word for me. I favor a tasty portmanteau as much as the next peckish etymologist, but "brunch" sounds a shade too yacht club. Clearly this is a remnant of personal hang-ups tied to milking cows and running a manure spreader before heading directly to church, coupled with the very foreign concept of lingering over any meal before noon. I should really get over these reverse pretensions especially since last night I was up at 1 a.m. eating potato chips on the couch while binging-watching a documentary on European auto racing, hardly a working class move. Furthermore—back to brunch—our elder daughter was home from her summer college course, and I am not so caught up in my self-centered conceits as to dismiss the simple joy of letting the late mid-morning unwind over a table laden with good food surrounded by the whole darn family and busy hummingbirds. Nor was my contentment diluted by the presence of the young gentleman currently keeping company with our elder daughter. He seems a pleasant and well-intended fellow possessed of enough wisdom to help with the dishes and casually mention that he has a job.

The Saturday evening previous to brunch, we enjoyed a country music concert courtesy of a longtime friend. He worked and played his way into the business a long, long time ago but still spends the bulk of his year commuting around the nation in a big shiny bus. When he's playing within range of our farm, he drops a line, and we meet up. This time his schedule and logistics allowed him to actually drop by the property for two hours between soundcheck and showtime. We sat on camp chairs overlooking the garden and the valley below, catching up and marveling at the green of it all. We covered some of the more troublesome topics of our times, but sometimes worry is just you revving in neutral, so we also told some stories on ourselves and enjoyed sitting so near the cucumber vines we could hear their leaves scritching in the breeze. Later that evening when we watched our friend at work on a stage overlooking tens of thousands of vociferous and well-oiled humans, the contrast was thunderous but no less wondrous.

Now it is Tuesday evening. I am closing up the chicken coop for the night having drawn no grand conclusions. This morning another billion-aire rode into space. Wildfire smoke stains the moon. The hummingbirds are at rest, waiting for dawn and whatever world we leave them.

Redeye

I caught the redeye out of L.A. mainly because that's something
I've always wanted to say, though truth be told I hopped off the plane in
Minneapolis, whereas if I really wanted to talk smart I shoulda rode all
the way to NYC like a true bicoastal hotshot.

As it is I'm back on Central time and a little logy.

I spent the bulk of my trip in a hotel room next to a dog in a hotel
room. I worked on my typing, he worked on his barking. I never saw him,
but I heard him and now and then his owner, barking back. Happily, each
day by bedtime everything settled to silence. Plus the sheets were clean,
the shower worked, and the price was right. Do the math, that's four out
of five stars.

The trip included a business meeting held a long ways from my
hotel after dark atop a rooftop garden with the Sunset Strip at our
feet and downtown Los Angeles in the flat sparkling distance. It was
the kind of clubhouse filled with people who are "famous-adjacent," and
what first registers as a sense of not fitting in slowly shifts to a sense of
how happy you are you didn't wind up in a joint like this until after you
were already past your "fitting in" years, and instead you can just focus
on enjoying the graciousness of your host, the business talk, and the
pan-roasted broccoli, which if I am not mistaken was done up in duck
fat, which can render retread truck tire shavings into a delicious fritter.
In the category of no longer flailing to fit in, these days I find it easier
to brazenly admit my appreciation of things like pan-fried broccoli and

deal with the fallout later, possibly while enjoying two pickled eggs and a Slim Jim. You can try too hard in either direction.

The meeting was collegial, but there is nothing to report, as is often the case in these things. I have been this far before, and here I still am. By the time you read this I will be packing the van for a trip to give a talk at the Oneida County Fair. I haven't chosen my outfit yet, but it won't look much different than the one I wore to the rooftop garden. At a certain age it is best to just be you, and hope you works.

I learn this lesson over and over. The same guy who caught the redeye in from L.A. also wanted to tip the airport shuttle driver real smooth like they do in movies or like the people were doing in valet parking outside that Sunset Strip joint, but I couldn't find my fives and wound up fumbling around counting out ones so clumsily I managed to drop my wallet, which the driver picked up off the blacktop and handed back to me, a kindness which should have earned him another solid dollar but by then I was all out of singles and madly sweating, so I just handed him the crumpled ones and drove myself home to nap.

Fair Gig

They got real happy weather for the Oneida County Fair, which was nice because I lugged my book and t-shirt boxes through sunshine rather than mud. They had a nice stage setup, too, and the sound technician had everything all plugged in and good to go.

I have said it before but I cannot say it enough: Always thank the sound technician. Out of politeness, of course, but also because on that board before them, every sound technician has what we figuratively refer to as the SUCK button. Peeve the sound tech, and you will suddenly come out of the speakers all a-garble, and people will wonder why you never enunciate.

Amplified enunciation is a big deal when you tell stories at a county fair, because there are competing noises, and what kind of fair would it be without them? Happily, this weekend's tent was located such and the microphone set so that the only background noise of any consequence came from a ride I will call the Centrifugally Undulating Barf-Slinger, and those screams didn't last long.

I was fetching the last box of T-shirts from the van when I heard a man say, "C'mere! I need to talk to you!" He sounded angry, so I was relieved when I turned and saw he was addressing a different man. They were both deeply tanned like you would be if you worked county fairs all summer, and sure enough they hunkered down between two trailers in the carnival crew parking area.

It being none of my business, I turned back to mine, but still heard the first man speaking in a heated cadence. "Yer not 14 years old anymore!

Yer gonna be dealin' with idiots like that every day! So you better figure it out!" It seems there had been a customer service issue. I snuck a glance as I headed back for the stage, and the guy who wasn't 14 anymore had gone off to pace beneath a tree and speed-drag a cigarette.

I had a little set list of stories I was gonna tell, but right off the bat I got off track—then again tangents are where the fun is. Being a little nervous in front of a tent full of people when no one—yourself included—knows where you're headed or how you'll get back to where you started is invigorating and focuses your attention even when the scent of fresh cheese curds drifts across the podium.

When it was over and the last book was signed, two long-lost friends showed up to help me pack up and load out. Sometimes life gives you roadies. Then the fair organizer handed me a coupon worth $10. I opted not to spend it on the rotating barf-slinger and instead loaded up on a giant tray of deep-fried cheese curds for the road. They were sizzling, salty, and squeaky—in other words, sublime. For the next three hours Wisconsin was beautiful through the windshield, and then I was home. Now I'm working off those curds. We're all living out our tangents. Somewhere out there I hope that carnival worker's day ran low on idiots.

Running Trail

The blackberries hung like grape clusters so I paused on my trail run to pick and eat them on the spot. Some may interpret this as a lack of dedication to my training regimen, but when life dangles fresh fruit in front of your face, you take a break at the buffet, and anyways, the Olympics are over.

Of course the best berries were just out of reach. To get at them I high-stepped and toe-wove my way through the leafy green canes. Even under the best of circumstances, I am no ballerina, let alone in navigating a briar patch, and when I set out to run again, my calves were scored and bleeding, but those berries were worth it.

Three strides into the resumption of my run, I felt a different discomfort and looked down to discover my shoes, socks, and worst of all the inner aspects of my shorts were studded with stick-tights, specifically the fruits of the alleged Virginia stickweed, which cling like BBs rolled in fiberglass and fish teeth and discharged from the devil's own shotgun. Their removal occupied me for some time. There were certain contortions, and I can only hope I didn't activate the neighbor's game camera.

I finished plucking and got back to running. The trail winds through mixed stands of trees, through hills and valleys, and in and out of the canopy cover. Deep in the trees the air was cool and moist with the recent rains; out on the open stretches the sun hit hot and the air went thick. It was the kind of day when the hay won't dry. Been years now since I last split twine and kicked alfalfa flakes down the manger, but still we see the present from the perspective of where we began.

I hit the uphills hard, and the look was more bovine than gazelle, but I've been running hills a lot lately and can heffalump right along. As I understand it, "power forward" is a basketball term, but in my case it's the only option.

As I came heaving up the final incline, I surprised a coyote, colored this time of year nearly fox red. It spun and loped a backtrack, then ducked into the goldenrod. The trail was a straight shot home now, directly along the spine of the ridge. After days of haze, the continental smoke plume had cleared, and I could see for miles, one of those views that makes you wonder why we can't all get along. Astronauts know what I'm talking about.

The open country, the open air, the sun, the sweat…it all put me in a spirit of purity, a spell broken shortly thereafter when I ate four oatmeal raisin cookies from a gas station, which was not part of the plan, but just like those blackberries, there they were, and furthermore, in light of my bleeding calves I felt it only responsible to guard against anemia.

MICHAEL PERRY

CHICKEN DIVESTITURE

FOR SOME TIME NOW I have been threatening to divest of the chickens. Threatening in this case is actually just grumpy mumbling, although yesterday when I snagged my fingers in the mesh while untangling the portable fence, I may have approached something on the level of a tantrum. It passed in a flash, but it did flash.

In fact it's not about the fence, nor is it about the chickens. This is our fourteenth year in the amateur poultry business. We have enjoyed a steady supply of eggs, often with dozens to spare and sometimes to sell. Also, barter-wise, a "couple dozen" eggs will get you some favors around these parts. And asparagus.

Fourteen years, and I still find it a form of mild magic to discover the nesting box shavings studded with not only your classic white eggs, but others in shades of brown, blue, aqua, and speckle. And from those shells when you crack them—especially during the months when the birds are out on grass, bugs, and other green goodies—slides a yolk of hearty yellow, sometimes two.

There is much I would miss if we took a year off. Even though we are down to a flock of less than twenty (springtime ran heavy to varmints), the sight of them hustling down the gangplank to peck away at the day always makes me feel better about the basics. And of an afternoon, the sight of that coop in the sun buoyed by the sound of a celebratory egg-lain cackle on the wind imbues the land with a sense of purpose. Those chickens are not feeding the world, but they are feeding a few of us.

Then there is "the chicken bucket," an empty ice cream pail full of every kitchen and table scrap. The birds spot it dangling from your hand as soon as you emerge from the porch and come for it on the run, their teeter-totter gait evidence they are nothing but feathered mini–tyranno-sauruses. We can switch over to composting, sure, but chickens are the epitome of efficiency. In go the bits, out comes food or fertilizer.

More fundamentally, the "chicken chores," as they are known around the family, have provided our children with a baseline understanding of the relationship between labor and having stuff. Gathering eggs and cleaning the coop now and then doesn't hold a candle to the ag-life their mother and I experienced (as we have told them many times and their eye-rolling will affirm) but link it to stacking firewood and you make a few inroads. Also, any child who learns to glove up and brave a pecking hen has a tiny head start on grading, facing, and overcoming life's obstacles.

In summary, I do not wish to ditch the chickens because of the chickens. Rather this is a case of life stages and schedules. The fact is, even with terrific chicken-sitting neighbors (one types and utters the phrase "chicken-sitting neighbors" with care), the birds require *arrangements*, and above all, time. Time that is not always mine, or ours.

We have entered initial hand-off negotiations with one of the above-referenced neighbors. We'll see how things go. I have reached that stage of life in which I am working on not doing things *just because*. Especially if those things have provided light entertainment and fresh scrambles for fourteen years.

I will miss most the ritual of closing the coop at night. Countless times I have stood beside the coop up there on the ridge, the birds roosted and secure within, and raised my eyes from the horizon to the sky. I take stock of the situation, the self, and the stars. The stars at least are steady, and that is enough.

Michael Perry

SPLITTER

It was a lush and sunbaked day, but somehow I still wound up in a brain wallow. I hail from a culture of walk it off and work it off but have come to understand this line of thinking is not universally helpful and in some cases, deadly. Earlier in the day I had been in communication with a farmer helping other farmers find safe harbor from the dark seas of depression. You can't work off what won't leave.

So when I grabbed the splitting axe and headed for the ridge where the loggers left a coffee-table sized slice of oak trunk lying flat in the weeds, I knew better than to think I was being so-called manly or effecting a cure; I was simply banking on sun and sweat to reset my system.

We have a motorized hydraulic splitter, and it works a treat, but this hunk of oak was too big for me to hoist aboard without first assembling a strike team consisting of an orthopedist, a chiropractor, a sports psychologist, and a bathtub's worth of liniment.

And yah, for you splitter specialists, I can indeed pull a pin and put the rig to work in the vertical, but this little venture was not about efficiency. Nor did I wish it to be muffled by ear plugs and fouled by exhaust. Visible from my worksite were—apart from a scattering of silver silo caps—several hundred square miles of undulating green capped by an infinity of blue. While I'm all for internal combustion, today's goal was not to use it, but defuse it.

As I measured the first strike, I noted rust on the axe head. It had been a while, which may be why we wound up here. Nothing to do, then, but knock that rust off.

The first strike terminated with a sodden *tunk*. This dispelled any residual manliness foolishness. I struck again. Another *tunk*, but this time accompanied by a *crack-rip*. There was hope. On the third strike the axe cleaved just like in the dictionary, and a fine slice of wood flipped into the weeds.

One does not sustain a readership by delivering literal blow-by-blow narratives of chopping oak stumps, so we fast forward an hour and—after the obligatory moment of backing off three steps to admire the accumulated pile—the walk back to the house, the axe dangling from one hand, the sweat soaking my shirt, nothing cured including the world, but feeling just a tad more muscular against whatever was sapping me and with a few day's winter warmth to boot. Less working it off than working it through.

Lest I cast myself too much as a reflective backwoods purist, I also took a set of before-and-after pictures (of the tool and materials, not of me) and posted them on social media. I got some likes, but not enough to set up an offshore account and retire. My career as an influencer has come up short of the stratosphere. But as far as I could see, the air was clear, and so too my head.

MICHAEL PERRY

Field Trip

I PICKED UP MY EIGHT-YEAR-OLD GODSON at his grandparent's house knowing it was my duty to entertain him for much of the next 48 hours. Above all the boy loves baseball, so I scheduled time for us to play hit and catch down at the neighbor's farm ball field, but as baseball is neither my avocation nor my forté, I knew I'd need some filler.

Unbeknownst to my traveling companion I had reserved a bulldozer. I have connections. I know some people.

Within twenty minutes of our arrival the youngster was ear-muffed and blading dirt and trash wood under the careful guidance of the dozer's owner in the seat beside him. My godson has not been raised a rough-neck, so I knew not what to expect, but his fully engaged gaze and hyp-notic half-grin suggested we were on the right track, an assessment con-firmed by his beaming thumbs-up when the ride concluded.

Next it was off to inspect a sawmill, where he set to cleaning saw-dust off the sawyer's platform. Then a towering deer stand set atop three telephone poles caught his eye, and it was off across the forty to climb the ladder. We paused en route to sample soybeans off the stem. The boy had never seen them in that state. It was great fun to watch his eyes widen at the reveal when I popped the first fuzzy green pod. He surprised me when he said they tasted good.

The deer stand provided a fine view and an introduction to raccoon poop. Then it was back across the forty to sit in a miniature two-seater biplane made from a large plastic drum, soup cans, and genuine aircraft fabric. Also reviewed were a log skidder, an excavator, and a dump truck.

Then a *real* airplane in a nearby hangar, although the pilot was not available. Maybe next time we fly.

After a tour of an informal skull and antler museum and a peek through a spotting scope, we headed out on a footpath that led us down to a creek, where for the next hour the youngster played nonstop with water and a stick, proving once again that the basics are best.

Next we stopped at a barn with a hay mow, the best sort of gymnasium. We also visited a boutique lumbering operation where the proprietor demonstrated a wood planer, and when the boy waded barefoot through the shavings, he recognized them as the same we use to line our chicken coop nesting boxes, which, the moment he and I returned home, he ran to and raided for all of their eggs, this for him being a novelty not a chore.

By the time he was packing up to leave two days later we had fed the neighbors' ducks and koi, played a solid hour of apple golf followed by apple batting practice, played guitar, toured the back forty (more deer stands!), and hauled a load of firewood. This doesn't even address the time spent in games and reading and adventures with his auntie and his cousin.

I am not writing to claim credit for the richness of our field trip. Rather I am writing my gratitude for the richness of those around me and their willingness to share of that richness through experience.

Around the time my godson was climbing into the minivan to leave I realized we hadn't made it to the baseball field. Somehow it never came up.

POTATOES

WE DUG POTATOES ALL AFTERNOON then at suppertime stood on the deck surveying the spread of boxes and buckets in the yard and took turns guessing their net weight. The early estimates ranged from an obviously low 50 pounds to the mid-200s. I had run one of the potato forks for hours so I had an up-close sense of the volume. I also like to think I have a certain intuition for these things. "Three hundred and fifty pounds," I said when it was my turn. Then I squinted at the boxes again. "No, wait, three-seventy-five."

My brother-in-law took last guess. He is an engineer who works in medical research and development. In short, he is a bit of a brain, the only evident weakness between his ears being an inexplicable loyalty to the Minnesota Vikings, an aberration eased by his pleasant demeanor, a willingness to pitch in and dig potatoes, and the Packers usually winning.

He scanned the accumulated containers. Then he mused aloud about the dimensions of each box, the volume of a five-gallon bucket, and the relative water weight of a potato. I rolled my eyes and made some wise-crack about Avogadro's number. He responded by reciting it deep into its decimals, then went back to sizing up spuds.

Finally he spoke. "Five hundred pounds."

It had been a fine day. Sun but not blazing sun. Breezy so no bugs. My father-in-law and I ran the potato forks, my brother-in-law and my elder daughter collected the potatoes. The rest of the friends and family harvested tomatoes, tomatillos, basil, beans, onions, zucchini, kale, chard, parsley, eggplant, and whatever else was ready. At one point our two daughters plucked the last of the plums from the tree we planted when the younger was born. Time is a merciless rocket sled.

My wife was the primary driver of this year's garden, but it was planted and tended throughout the summer with the steady help of friends and family. No one keeps a spreadsheet, but helpers are welcome to take what they wish. And on days like the potato harvest, the benefits extend beyond the gathering of food to the gathering itself. Nieces and nephews splashing in the wading pool, rest breaks beneath the shade of the maple, happily fierce games of cornhole, some Frisbee, stories thrice-told, and then, at the end, a big meal on the deck, the fresh produce supplemented by grilled burgers and sausage, cold drinks, and a solid sense of accomplishment.

And, of course, the potato poundage guessing game. My wife had pre-weighed the goods while we were cleaning up, so after my brother-in-law submitted his overwrought estimate we all turned to her.

"Five hundred and twenty pounds," she said.

You know how every once in a while the Vikings do beat the Packers? And then you have to face your purple-proud friend? The one you've been teasing all week? I took my medicine with a smile. The scoreboard says what the scoreboard says.

Summer is winding down. Should you attend some fall festival and find yourself at one of those booths where you guess how many jelly beans are in the jar, and this tall bespectacled fellow in a Vikings hoodie eases up beside you, maybe sit that round out. Rather, go have a nice baked potato. There's lots.

MUSHROOMING

LAST WEEK MY FRIEND FRANK AND I went mushroom hunting in our woods. Conditions converged to provide a profusion of fungi, and it seemed we stopped every few feet to review a fresh specimen. Orange, white, gray, golden, spotted, stippled, plain, smooth, rough, flaky, stemmed, and shelved, growing out of the trees or growing out of the duff, they were popping out all over.

I don't know diddly about mushroom hunting. I can identify the very obvious morel and just this year have solidified my ability to distinguish between chicken-of-the-woods and hen-of-the-woods, but this level of proficiency is akin to identifying a beach ball in a tub full of golf balls. If I authored a mushroom hunter's guidebook, it would be three pages long and scrawled in fat crayon.

Frank, on the other hand, can identify numerous mushrooms, although more than once when I led him to a cluster he said, "I *think* that one is edible," or "I don't *think* you can eat that one," which means I don't *think* he's quite ready for his own YouTube channel. That said, I kept a close eye on him and every time he invoked *think*, he left the mushroom be. The best antidote to eating a poisonous mushroom is to not eat the poisonous mushroom.

In theory we were foraging, but we were also happily shooting the breeze. We have known each other for years but tend to see each other only a time or two per year. Our families get on well, and we usually wind up around a fire pit or sharing a meal. On this day our time was short, but in addition to the mushroom hunt and general visiting we managed a rousing game of kubb. I enjoy kubb, although I once landed myself in hot water with some of its leading local aficionados when I referred to it as "hippie horseshoes." I delivered my apology in person.

Uphill, downhill, sidehill, we ranged across twenty or so acres, chattering as we meandered, eyes to the forest floor and to stumps and to decaying deadfalls. While we are generally encouraged to hold our heads high and take in the beauty surrounding us, there is much richness to be observed amongst the rotting leaves and fallen pine needles underfoot.

I was looking in another direction when I heard Frank exclaim, "Ohhhh!" and sure enough, he'd found a good one, a county fair prize-sized hen-of-the-woods nestled up against a stump like an actual fat napping chicken. Carefully he severed it with his knife and tucked it in a paper shopping bag for the trip home. He declared it was the kind of find that would make his day even if it was the only mushroom he found. But we stuck with it a while longer, and he also collected some edible puffballs and a lovely orange-tinged chicken-of-the-woods.

Before Frank and his family departed, we loaded them up with produce from our garden. Then we stood around their car and took a while to say good-bye. All told, it was a visit of just a few hours, and there is not much more to report except that joy is good people joining together in open air and my wife is a kubb assassin.

LAMBEAU

THE WISPY SKITTER underlying today's breeze is a note passed beneath the screen door advising that the birch leaves have begun to slip their summer stems. It is at once a poetic rustle and a prosaic reminder to fetch the storm door from the pole barn.

Less subtly, autumn was also announced last night by a chorus of 77,240 voices raised in praise of the Green Bay Packers.

I was happy to be among them.

This Lambeau visit came courtesy of my wife, who cultivates friends who think of her when they find themselves privy to a pair of passes. My wife in turn was kind enough to invite me. It was our second ever trip to the house Vince and Curly built. We treated it as a date night, lucky us.

My affection for Green Bay Packers football is the manifestation of many things. Generally, it is drawn from my experiences playing the game gleefully as a young man. It is the pleasure of watching professionals play the game at a level of which I can only dream. It is the blend of intricate patterns and blunt force, of the glorious spiraling arc and the goofball bad bounce, of the brainy scheming and the brawny bulldozing.

Specifically to the beloved Pack, I revel in a symbol around which we cheeseheads can all still largely unite, even in these fractious times. That is to say if you encounter someone sporting that squashed "G" you know the two of you share at least one point of allegiance. The madness of mobs is well documented and best avoided, unless that mob is chanting "Go, Pack, Go!" in which case I joyfully join in. On any given Monday, I like to think I am a sensible fellow, but come Monday Night Football,

I like to think my 77,239 roaring seatmates and I were essential in confounding the best-laid plans of the Detroit Lions offense. Decibels are defense.

All things considered, I am plumb happy to observe the Packers from my couch. Football is perfectly designed for our high-def multi-cam times. But how breathtaking it was to be a present witness as Aaron Rodgers uncorked a fifty-yarder to Davante Adams or bulleted a touch-down into a double-coverage window the size of the box that ball came in or to turn to a stranger and exult when the ball disappeared amongst the feet of the big men and emerged held aloft by one clad in green and gold. Some art forms are not meant to be parsed, they are to be cheered with fist pumps.

It was late when we finally cleared the postgame traffic backup and hit highway speeds. It would be nearly 2 a.m. before we got home. When I stopped to gas up in Wausau, everyone at the pumps was wearing Pack-ers gear with the exception of a single sad soul in Honolulu blue. On my way to get coffee I gave him a solid and friendly nod, as I am well past the age of starting parking lot fights based on laundry, plus you see a Lions fan, you see someone living out a dedication that on some level can only be admired. As for the rest of us, we were tired with miles to go and by dawn would be back to our dailies and differences, and who knows what autumn and the schedule will bring, but even as we shuffled to the check-out, the roar resonated: Go, Pack, Go.

Fool for Football

ONE TRIES TO AVOID writing about the same thing two weeks in a row, especially something so fleeting as a National Football League game, but when Mason Crosby kicked the Packers to last-second victory last Sunday night, I leapt around the living room like a thunderous third grader, and so to prolong those echoes of joy I am allowing myself to revisit the topic in general.

I have come to enjoy the NFL mostly in terms of following characters in a soap opera, the only reliable reality being the sixty minutes of live play, where there is no faking anything other than the occasional punt, and meritocracy triumphs except when the oblong ball goes trickster or referees overdo the legalese.

There is a temptation to denigrate certain athletes as spoiled, pampered and overpaid, but rarely does that standard of scrutiny extend to the skybox. What is a free agent but a free marketeer? Furthermore, on a day when Mason Crosby and several other kickers delivered booming (and in one case, record breaking) last-chance victories, my appreciation for their professionalism was bolstered by the fact that I too used to kick field goals.

My personal record was a 42-yarder. That's only 24 yards short of the fresh record set last Sunday when the Ravens shell-shocked the Lions at the end of regulation. I should note I kicked mine with the wind and without pads or opposition, it departed the tee at an angle that would have sent it smack into the center's hinder, and when it did go through the uprights it was wobbling like a molting vertigo-stricken duck, and you couldn't have snuck a Skoal can between the crossbar and the pigskin.

I disabused myself of the last lingering illusions that I was good enough to be a pampered pro years ago during a stretch when my work took me to several NFL training camps and on the sidelines for a real game. When Pittsburgh Steelers running back Jerome "The Bus" Bettis ran out of bounds beside me I felt a palpable wave of displaced air and a series of non-metaphorical geologic tremors. While standing in the tunnel during pregame introductions, I turned to my right only to have my view blocked by a hairy tree trunk which, as I tipped my head back and traced the trunk to its source, turned out to be the left bicep of Bruce—uncle to Clay—Matthews. Perhaps most startling was the day I ate lunch with a group of offensive linemen. I like to think of myself as a real meat and potatoes guy, but once you've watched a pulling guard devour a pile of meat the size of a badger, you lose your appetite for cutback blocks.

And then there were the little things: Down on the sidelines of a game between the Steelers and the Titans (perhaps then still the Oilers), every time his offense got within a certain yardage of the end zone, I watched as placekicker Al Del Greco walked off to a corner of the field and practiced his leg swing. In the fourth quarter I eased over to where he was shadow-kicking and noted a bare spot the size of a nickel worn into the grass, which spoke to the microscopic consistency of his craft.

Lastly, one day at practice I stood on the fifty-yard line as quarterback Elvis Grbac stood on the goal line and zinged footballs over my head. They passed through the air with an audible buzz.

Sometimes I still lurch from the couch and declare "I coulda caught/kicked/hit that!" Then I settle back to the cheese dip, knowing, No I couldn'ta, and instead I can say what we said last week and—win or lose—will say again next week: Go, Pack, Go.

Swing Set, Swung Set

This week on a whim I demolished the old swing set.

It was long past time.

Based on neighborhood historians we know this set had been hosting clambering kids for at least 25 years. It was a galvanized "T-swing" model bolted together from a kit and included swings, a set of horizontal monkey bars, and a slide. By the time we moved onto the property the slide was slightly off-kilter, and one swing seat (or maybe the trapeze?) was missing. But whenever tots hit the yard, they converged on the set, often at a dead run straight from the minivan.

The T-bar ends of the swing always made me shudder as they were pre-safety cap and positioned right at temple level for this grownup. I always imagined I'd walk into one of them while mowing the lawn and scallop my scalp. Clearly I was never worried enough to take the time and actually cap them.

Over the years, through family reunions, fire ring get-togethers, informal drop-ins, and long gardening days, the swing stood square and solid. A touch of rust here and there, and that slide never did set straight and in fact twisted a little more over time, but the whole works remained functional. Then a few winters past, a white pine branch snapped under snow load and knocked the non-slide end cattywampus.

And yet still it stood.

And still the kids climbed and swung.

It looked goofy out there in the yard, half-crushed and drunkenly aslant, but in solving the relevant equation for joy and aesthetics, joy won.

I considered trying to straighten it using the tractor and loader, but it was clear the piping was likely to snap on the rebound, so I let it be. By then several of the kids who used to ask for a lift up to the monkey bars were ducking to pass beneath them, and if they did still climb up and sit at the top of the slide, their feet would have extended three-quarters of the way down.

Then came the day this spring when the crease at the base of one of the bent pipes rusted through just enough that a clambering child cracked it the rest of the way. Now one whole end of the swing swayed loosely. The kids still climbed the other end, but at some point even the joy equation cannot out-factor the safety equation. After everyone was gone, I got the tractor and the loader, lifted the swing from the earth (whoever planted it did an admirable job of sinking the base in cement), and placed it on the scrap iron pile.

The demolition was eased by the fact that we have a terrific back-up—a towering vintage model I found on Craigslist and salvaged from a schoolyard in Rochester, Minnesota. Upon arrival I discovered the top pipe was fourteen feet longer than the truck bed. There was an incident in a traffic circle and my driver's license and heart nearly didn't survive the trip home. Later my trucker brother enumerated the violations I would have incurred had I encountered the DOT. But we got it planted, and with its four seats suspended by chains you could drag logs with, it will more than take up the slack for joy.

We are all lengthening shadows cast by a sinking sun, sang the prophet Ray Wylie Hubbard just now as I was writing this, and raising my eyes to the freshly bare spot in the lawn where the swing stood all those years, I think of the children happily playing on it right to the day it cast its final shadow, and the deal is, that was a swing well swung.

FISHING FALLOUT

THE FIRST FIRE OF THE SEASON is whirling in the woodstove, the sidewinding flames feeding on the open draft, the room air tinged with the ozone scent of a summer's dust scorching off. As I sit down across the room to write this column, I can already feel the warmth slow-rolling the chill. I'll leave it to blaze until it sets a good solid stoke, then dial it down to a slow burn.

A friend of mine once composed a song including the lyric, "I go for the caste/I fall off a bass boat." At first listen, the invocation of a bass boat—let alone toppling from one—seems a pratfall non sequitur, as the song is neither a novelty number nor an anthem to sport fishing. In fact, it's a heavy song about heavy issues, as implied by the intentional use of "caste" rather than "cast."

The song spun through on a random mix as I was setting the fire today. It's a powerful piece of work, and I am happy to report I am able to feel the song framed in that power.

But also sometimes I just giggle. Because the first time I heard the bass boat lyric, in a YouTube clip posted by a fan at a live show, I utterly missed the point, context, and nuanced spelling and instead thought, "Hey! I too went for the cast and fell off a bass boat!"

It was opening day of fishing season. I'm not sure which year. I know I was at least in college, possibly even graduated. My father and I rowed a flat-bottomed john boat up a creek to the far end of a shallow lake lurky with northern pike. While an engineless john boat is not technically a bass boat, that's what we mostly caught in it early on, so I invoke both poetic license and fisherman's privilege in the telling of this tale.

It was a cold day, gray and windy. Much like today, and thus the fire over there across the room. Which needs modulating, I see. Be right back.

Three sticks added and the damper damped. We return now to the wave-slapping lake, where against all training and better judgment and in hopes of slinging my lure to the far reaches of a weedy cove, I stood up in the boat, rared back, and two-armed the cast with all the whip I could muster.

At which point the pole snapped, throwing me off balance. I teetered and windmilled at the edge of the boat, the busted rod and reel arcing out of my hand and into the drink.

The angle of my teeter was such that even as I windmilled I knew I would shortly be swimming. *My father!* I thought. *He will save his firstborn son!* I turned my wide eyes toward him.

He was high-speed reverse crab-walking to the high side of the boat, dangling not so much as a finger my way.

In I went.

I resurfaced making a sound evocative of a panicking asthmatic calf. As Dad bravely and dryly counterbalanced at the opposite end of the boat, I scrambled aboard. Then I rowed all the way back just to counter the teeth-chattering wind cutting through my sopping togs. Dad kept fishing.

I have needled my father about this incident for years. In his defense it was a shallow lake. Also, as he kept fishing while I soggily rowed, he snagged my line and got my lure and reel back. And as soon as we got home, he stoked up the woodstove so I might warm myself beside it.

A cold autumn day, an oddball lyric, a crackling fire, all blending to summon a long-gone spring day and a smile. Memories will not save us, but they will warm us.

Moon Moves

THE FULL MOON EASED UP a sulky orange. Later when I walked out to close the chicken coop, it was white and riding high. An elongated cloud hung between it and the earth, illuminated and ghostly, a strand of carded wool. Somewhere invisibly above, a flock of geese honked. It is my understanding they take to the night air because it is cool and smooth and not bumpy with daytime thermals. It seemed they were headed north, but I trust they'll figure it out.

I stood beside the coop as I have done I suppose several thousand times since we moved to this farm, a ceremonial and practical appointment marking the end of day but maintained primarily to keep the fox from the henhouse, to say nothing of weasels, skunks, raccoons, and fishers.

As is often the case on a night as still as this, I could hear the semis running the interstate two miles distant, the steady flow of commerce propelled by diesel through darkness, the running lights sliding along at ground level while geese beat the air above.

For a decade or so stretch back there in the early days, I spent swathes of time on the road with truckers, writing about their lives and trade, taking notes from the shotgun seat. I can pause beside the garden, stripped and set for the fallow season but for a few pumpkins and the hearty kales and chards, and visualize the glow of the dashboard, the easy rise and fall of the air-ride cab, the concrete super slab perpetually spilling into view beneath the headlight flow. I feel myself traveling even as I stand here.

I drop the pocket door and elicit not a cluck. The chickens are at roost and at rest, leaving the wild geese to do their thing. A chicken is bound to migrate between the feed pail and the nesting box, with peck-and-scratch side trips as the fencing allows, but beyond that they are homebodies, upshot being it is easier to find the eggs.

It's back up the rise then, to the crest of the hill and the house, remembering to duck beneath the bare branches of the apple tree, as nothing harshes the lunar ceremonial scene like stick to the eye. A last look at the moon, then it's inside to lock the door and climb the stairs, call it a day.

Tomorrow there will be bills and appointments, errands and I imagine some missteps, backtracking, and low-key futility. I will probably try to open my office door without unlocking it even though it has to be unlocked every morning, and this will render me testy at the only person to blame, the same person who knows where the key is stashed and in fact was the last to stash it, but nonetheless requires the dumb surprise of the failed entry to remind him to actually use said key. Again, this is likely to be only the first setback of the day.

For now, however, it is head to the pillow, mind to the sky, choose your drift-off adventure: Take a trip to the moon, sit astride a sparse cloud, fly point with the midnight geese. And failing that, throw open the window to allow the sound of the highway in, all those miles you banked all those years ago unspooling in memory for you now, the moon slowly edging its way toward morning.

MICHAEL PERRY

Los Angeles Again

I COMPOSE THIS NOTE on a return flight from Los Angeles where I didn't pick up a lot of actionable advice other than if you hope to catch a ride out the back door of SoFi Stadium at 1:30 a.m. you would be better off not to. Rather, go ahead and hike right out past Touchdown Drive to Pincay Drive, then hustle up to the little turnaround just off Carlton which is where the last of the orange cones and world-weary security guards make their final stand. You'll know you're headed in the right direction if you see other wee-hour stragglers wandering heads-down, tapping at their ride-hailing apps like perplexed zombies.

I learned this all on the fly and the flop. After inviting driver number one, I watched our blue dots zig-zag back and forth, nearing but never quite reaching each other. Our correspondence—now immortalized in my iPhone—took on the desperate tone of two people trying to work out a long-distance relationship until finally the driver said it just wasn't worth it anymore and ghosted me. It gave me flashbacks to my young dating career, only with postcards and long distance phone calls. The second driver was more understanding, especially after I made that jog out to Carlton. He drove like a charioteer and delivered me shortly to my room.

This was my second trip to Los Angeles in four months. Both visits were for work that may or may not manifest. This time I was accompanied by my main business partner to whom I am also married. Between official meetings we ate seafood in a restaurant overlooking the Pacific near Topanga Canyon, which sounds exotic to a cheesehead except on this gray day the sea was whipped by wind and rain, and we could have been in Duluth when Lake Superior was feeling grumpy.

Earlier we sheltered from the rain in the Getty Villa Museum where a quick review of Greco-Roman funeraria reaffirmed that whatever ostentatious silliness we're up to now we've been up to forever, and we would do well to take ourselves and our most insistent declarations less seriously, because one way or the other it's all gonna wind up as dirt, dust, or trinkets in a gift shop.

On our one sunny day we walked and gawked at the Santa Monica and Venice Beach promenade. The glory and madness of the human cavalcade is elixir for a retiring loner such as I, shaking my little snow globe and forcing me to view the world through unfamiliar fractals. I include the grimmer things we saw. But to walk through it rather than scroll through it makes all the difference in the world. I enjoy needling city folk, but I stopped making fun of them a long time ago, mostly because in the midst of the multifarious scene I am reminded how stiff and worriedly I can hunch myself against things I've never met. Or grappled with.

I hope I have also learned that sometimes when you are a tourist you should act like a tourist, so on the final sunny evening we borrowed camp chairs and hiked the asphalt until we reached the beach, settled in with a book apiece, and resolved to take in the Santa Monica sea breeze and sunset, only to have our resolve dwindle in the teeth of that breeze, which did not match the view, and so again we strolled, watching on the move as the sun passed from view. As the molten bead shrank and snapped to nothing, a group of street performers broke into a loud cheer. We walked past them into dusk, two teensy fleeting links in the human chain.

LAST OF THE LEAVES

LAST NIGHT'S FROST trimmed back the chard, so you know it was the real deal. Jury's still out on the dinosaur kale. I'll swing back later in the afternoon for a sample and wellness check.

It's popular to mock kale, and I've made some hay in that regard myself, but once a day I like to snap off a frond and eat it during the walk back to the office. It tastes somewhere between cabbage and grass, both acceptable notes, and anyways, I've never minded eating my greens. I envision the chlorophyll infiltrating my cells, displacing the snacky sludge.

It was a chill, silent morning after a week of winds so ripping and persistent they scrambled our television signal. Sunday afternoon I felt like I was watching football on a flipbook. My wife said she was sorry I had to put up with that. She is known for speaking truthfully, but in this case the subtext was something along the lines of a verbal head-pat.

But now it was the workaday weekday, and I had wandered down to release the chickens. While filling their scratch pans I heard a papery *tick-tick*. I turned and located the source of the sound: pretty yellow leaves, letting loose of their own accord and dropping through a maple tree just outside the chicken run. Each *tick* conveyed the light collision of the leaf with a branch or another leaf. Only in that moment did I fully absorb how the morning air was at rest rather than rattling the tree limbs like skeleton castanets.

So I stood there and enjoyed the sound of free-falling leaves, not because I am some sort of naturalist aesthete, but because it seems when one has privileged access to a sound that delicate in an indelicate world one would do well to enjoy it in the moment while recording it to the ol' brain pan for future reference and situations less conducive to calm, perhaps as a meditation while at the dentist or during the din of a political advertisement.

It was time to release the chickens. I left the leaves and raised their little door. They emerged with a bit more reservation than usual, perhaps testing the temperature with their beaks. I opened a section of the fence so they could range out and get a taste of the waning weeds, maybe snap up a logy grasshopper.

Later that morning an odd motion caught my eye in the treeline downslope from the coop. A large brown bird was flapping in a wild apple tree. At first I thought a killer raptor was struggling to roost, and I started toward the door to intervene on behalf of the chickens. Then another bird joined the first. And then another, and another, until an entire flock of wild turkeys was flopping and teetering in the branches, all pecking at the last of the shrunken fruit. The tree wasn't built to hold two turkeys, let alone the dozen, so it was an entertaining scene, and I took time to enjoy it as I had the ticking leaves. Sometime later it occurred to me that the sound of those leaves reminded me of another quietness, that being the sound of snowflakes striking other snowflakes, a tone poem inbound soon enough.

Throwbackhoe

THIS WEEK I DUG OUT some snapshots from my days as a ranch hand in Wyoming. They were taken sometime between 1981 and 1986. There I stood wide-legged in the Western sun with no need to suck my belly in, confident in the way young people are that stance will overcome substance. Over time the pose becomes harder to hold.

But you gotta start somewhere. In my case, leaving home at the age of sixteen to run a hay swather. Back on the home farm in Chippewa County, we cut our hay in ever-shrinking concentric squares, sickling seven feet per pass. In Carbon County, Wyoming, they put me in a machine that cut twice that wide. Rather than make squares we ran up and back, and in some cases the windrows were a mile long. As I mowed the vast green sea, I felt I was captaining a galleon.

But all that tall grass won't grow if you don't water it, and from those four snapshots I am prompted to recall how my boss had sent my partner and me afield to replace culverts and irrigation spillways. That summer we built a lot of dams and water crossings using factory reject sewage tubing and manhole inspection chambers. The boss had a connection at the concrete plant, and he'd buy them by the truckload.

In one of the photos I'm using the front end loader of a backhoe tractor to unload one of the tremendously heavy tubes. One edge of the tube is resting on the flatbed semi trailer; the other edge is overlapping the hood of the tractor. The loader appears to be extended to maximum height. Can't raise it, can't lower it. I have some faint memory of being kinda stuck there, then dragging the tube off the trailer to swing like a pendulum, dropping it on the out-swing as it cleared the radiator. These are tactics not taught in your more reputable heavy equipment materials-handling courses. Also, OSHA would like a word.

But we were working a thousand acres from nowhere. No one to cite us, no one to save us. Before the day was done, we built several ditch crossings. I'd excavate the waterway with the backhoe, waller the tubes into place, then tap them together end to end using the hoe. Finally I'd use the loader to build and grade a dirt road across them.

In the final photo I'm using the backhoe to rip a wooden spillway from the earth. It strikes me now that it was probably built by hand and put in place with spades and pry bars long before I was born. And now here I am looking at images of myself that are suddenly vintage in their own right.

I tend to get into certain recursive grooves, and here lately it's been my steady hobby to reconsider reminiscence. To question the value of waxing dreamy about the past when the present requires so much attention. To ask if I should be burning time on times to which I cannot return.

But to reconsider reminiscence is not to reject it. I am happy to stand in my little typing room above the garage and let these four colored rectangles revive the sense memory of conducting honest work in the open air. To smile in recognition at my forgotten younger self knowing full well he was dumb and bluff but on the path. Not the path to perfection, but one along which he would come to know it is less about holding the pose than freeing the flow.

Winter Warning

Home for a weekend visit from college, our daughter parked her car in the yard prior to the first snow of the season. The next morning she was gone, leaving a green rectangle on a slate of white. There was the temptation to spin something metaphorically profound or tear-jerky from the image, but in fact she had taken her stuttering vehicle to a mechanic, and based on the update I just received, my sentimentality will be tempered by my checkbook.

To be fair, the scholar in question holds down a job and contributes a pre-agreed and not insignificant percentage of her own costs of living, tuition, and automotive expenses, so I will count my blessings as I balance the checkbook.

Fifty-six trips around the sun and yet last night when I stepped out beneath the yard light and saw that the snow was gonna stick, I felt the usual surprise. Autumn buffers us with leaves that change color over time, then drop to the ground in stages. Temperatures moderate, but you still get that odd hot day, or at the very least T-shirt weather.

And then one day it snows like this and winter says, I'm serious.

That is not to say winter is here to stay. It's likely things will melt back to brown. But that first white blanket is nature's way of announcing, Last chance to get them garden hoses in or there's a chance you won't see them 'til May. Also, what's yer snowplow status?

In another sign it's time to stop pretending we're not seasonally in for it, yesterday I stepped out of the office and embarked on an inadvertent ski trip. I was wearing my ancient foam rubber clogs, which are perfect for those quick trips between the house and the garage room where I work but were long ago worn treadless.

I made it to the bottom of the hill without crashing, but to conjure the appropriate mental image, picture an aging slalom racer who has been not so much hitting the slopes as the doughnuts and paddles the air like he's on the flight deck of an aircraft carrier trying to land the entire Blue Angels team simultaneously from different directions while riding a surfboard. And as he is not wearing goggles, you can see his very wide eyes.

In light of my low-end athleticism and high-end health insurance deductible, I went straight to the porch, dug out a pair of ice cleats, and mounted them on the clogs, where they will remain until the tulips bloom. Some will mock, but in the pursuit of balancing ease and utility, I maintain the combo of cleats and clogs is pretty much apex tech.

Sunday evening I drove my daughter to pick up her car, now repaired. We transferred her snowboard, clean laundry, and some home cooking from my vehicle to hers. Then I hugged her and followed her back to the highway where her taillights merged with all the others and curved out of sight. There's a shot the snow will be gone by mid-week, but out the window right now the green rectangle is still sharp, and sometimes you don't have to work a metaphor, just feel it.

Michael Perry

BLAZE ORANGE

My younger daughter is currently swooping to and fro on our big old swing set clad in a fluorescent orange vest and cap. If you're from where we're from I need not explain the color of the couture. If you're not from where we're from, well, it's deer hunting season and "blaze" or "hunter" orange is worn to ensure you are not mistaken for a whitetail. Blaze pink has also been recently approved, the more the merrier.

For specific cultural reasons I once requested a New York publisher place blaze orange accents on the cover of a book I wrote. I even went so far as to provide the award-winning book jacket designer with the proper Pantone code, which I procured courtesy of a graphic designer pal also raised in the Wisconsin northwoods, and who—even if he isn't a deer hunter—has likely inhaled his share of secondhand buck scent.

When the first proofs arrived from New York the accents were present, but in an anemic orange nowhere near matching the Pantone. As a reticent team player stricken with Midwestern nice and a heavy dose of impostor syndrome, I'm mostly a pushover in these situations, but in this instance I was speaking for my people and thus during the follow-up conference call gently pointed out to the award-winning book jacket designer that this was not the color I had specifically requested.

"Oh," said the man, "we don't think people will notice the difference." This was before the days of Zoom, but I could envision him waving his hand dismissively from a Midtown Manhattan skyscraper. It occurred to me that what you had right here was the very personification of the nation's cultural divide, and maybe this was my chance to break out of my

Midwestern shell to deliver a blistering jeremiad about the blithe dismissal of a permeant cultural marker just because you've never encountered it your own self.

Instead I just quietly explained that no, that's what we wear around here at a specific time of year for a very specific reason and even the non-hunters know that and also, Sir, have you never watched a Packers game?

I pause now to establish that New York City citizens have been most accommodating of me and my clodhopper demeanor, have supported my writing habit in ways I never dared dream, and have also nearly always paid for lunch—but now and then they betray certain assumptions and presumptions requiring me to blow their minds with the possibility that the curation of definitive style is not limited to the backstage bunch at Fashion Week.

On a corollary note, I have also been known to remind them with a smile that sometimes out here in the rural Midwest, we think things up *all by ourselves.*

Shortly I will be in my deer stand. I will not be carrying the book in question but am happy to report that if I wanted to I could, because after a series of polite negotiations the spine and cover were accented with a blaze orange hue meeting the standards set by the Wisconsin Department of Natural Resources deer hunting regulations handbook. I consider this a triumph of cultural intersection. Perhaps I will airmail some buck sausage.

Budgetary Concerns

In my marriage there is a rule: If one spouse is out and about and spots an object of desire (commercial, not carnal) the price of which meets or exceeds a certain amount, the coveting spouse is obligated to call or return home to discuss the matter with the other spouse for joint approval before dropping the dollars.

So it was that a month ago I found myself trying to convince my wife I needed a very special crossbow.

I made my pitch in the kitchen. I promised to take really good care of the crossbow, to use it as a means of provision, and…well, that was pretty much all I could come up with.

She regarded me with an expression I can only describe as terminal reservation. I felt lonely.

Then, rather than saying no, she began asking sensible questions. Nothing is more deadly in these circumstances than sensible questions. I parried weakly with the old foot-shuffle mumblemouth. Then I panicked and launched a Hail Mary response, revealing that one of my friends owned that exact model of crossbow, and we were thinking it would be good if I got the same one so we could share arrows should we ever wind up in the same bunker when It All Goes Down.

There followed a silence that absorbed all the energy of the earth. I recognized my fatal overreach for what it was and placed the crossbow on mental layaway.

And now this week I found out I can't buy the local Catholic church.

The church is in my hometown. I discovered it was for sale when I drove up north to go deer hunting with my brothers. The church was suppressed in 2003. That's the term the bishop used during the final ceremony; you could also say "shut down," although a loyal group of folks have kept it available for funerals and other gatherings. That loyal group (and, I assume, other resources) have dwindled. I would love to swoop in and scoop it up, and would if I could. It is one of the places that help me love that place. But at the moment, my own house needs attention in both the metaphorical and shingle sense. I also have one kid in college and one kid in braces. This focuses the budget.

Still, I checked the price and ran it past my wife. I may have mentioned turning it into a recording studio and robot building center and also keeping the funerals going. Having attended emotionally moving events there herself, she understands. But still she vetoed my dreams.

Wait: that's neither accurate nor fair. She never said no. In fact I don't think she has ever said no. You'll notice I've not quoted her invoking the words *forbid* or *forbade* or any version of same. My optimistic read here is that she respects my autonomy. My realistic read is she knows very well she doesn't have to say no, she just has to let me stand there and listen to myself.

FIREWOOD SLED

CHRISTMAS CAME EARLY for our teenage daughter this week. The local farm store had a sale on ice fishing sleds. I bought one, and in the very act of presenting it to her, committed an act of magic in which it transmogrified from an ice fishing sled into a wood-hauling sled.

Vainly I searched for the wonder in her eyes.

Our previous wood-hauling sled lasted over a decade before disintegrating. In fact we towed our current wood-hauling daughter in it as a swaddled bundle on Christmas tree hunts long before she ever dragged it across the yard filled with split oak. I suspect she longs for those tinier times, especially tonight as she leans into the wind and falling temperatures on her second trip to the shed for an extra load as buffer against the cold snap.

I have long sung the praises of firewood as a character-molding medium. In fact both daughters will identify this as one of my more well-worn choruses. I have of course shared with them the old Thoreauvian saw about firewood warming you twice—once when you split it and once when you burn it—although by now they know it warms us multiple times (when we cut it, when we split it, when we stack it, when we fetch it, when we burn it, when we argue about whose turn it is to fetch more).

Most winter days we can get by on a single sled full, but on colder, windier days I order up that second load. Both daughters learned early not to slump and complain lest I launch into remonstrations and recollections from a firewood-driven childhood, including Saturdays spent out back chonking chunks of slabwood into a hay wagon fitted with side racks.

We only had to get one load, but as opposed to the ice-fishing sled routine, this was a chore completed in hours, not minutes. Then the slabwood had to be thrown down a slide into the basement. Then stacked. And stacked. And stacked. And then carried back upstairs by the armload, day after day.

Oh, you can probably hear me, and you can probably see the child heading back into the snowy night with the sled, knowing it is easier to drag wood than listen to all that.

But then comes last night in the living room, me cutting up venison on a card table ('tis the season), my wife running a family meeting, and our teenaged daughter sitting before the fire she helped build, conversing with us in the way teens do—alternately silly, serious, and sparring—but conversing nonetheless. There was a warmth to the moment beyond the red coals behind the glass, and later both my wife and I would note it.

I stayed up well past midnight with the deer legs and was still asleep at dawn when I was knocked awake by a series of tumbling thuds, which I quickly identified as the sound of my daughter dumping a load of firewood beside the stove before leaving for school. It seemed the perfect teenaged way of letting dad know you did your chores.

Ice Fishing

Word is some of my acquaintances to the north are ice fishing. I wish them good luck and flotation.

My reservations about going out on the ice in our neck of the woods is tied to a specific recency bias, that being the sound of last weekend's blizzard dripping off the eaves and tonight's forecast, which includes thunderstorms and temperatures in the high 50s. I trust my friends have done their safety checks. Here's to them, and may they shortly be fileting and fryin' 'em up in a pan.

That last phrase descends from my Grandpa Peterson. "You just fry 'em up in a pan," he'd say, regarding the cooking of fish. This from a man who couldn't open a can of beans. I am not making this up. Favored among our treasured family anecdotes is the one about the time Grandma left for a few days and returned to find Grandpa sullen and hungry, the can opener on the counter beside the bean can, the tin cylinder mangled but unbreached, its contents untouched.

This same Grandpa Peterson also reassured us that we could catch fish using nothing but a willow switch, a length of thread, and an unclasped safety pin. Given enough starving fish I suppose this is true, but deep down inside I think Grandpa read about it in a book once and never actually field tested the recommendation. Neither did I, especially not after I got my first rod and reel from Grandpa Perry.

Grandpa Perry was the outdoors grandpa. He fished as much as you'd hope any grandpa would and often took us kids along. Knowing what I know now about putting yourself in a boat with kids slinging hooks, I admire both his love and bravery. That said, he spent some time on the beach in Iwo Jima during World War II, so his concept of danger was calibrated to a different standard than most.

It was with Grandpa Perry that I did most of my ice fishing. In the early days we made holes in the ice with a "spud," which was basically a giant chisel with a loop of rope attached to one end. You put your arm through the loop in case the spud broke through the ice and you lost your grip on it. In those days the spud was taller than I, and I remember wondering if it might not just pull me under the ice along with it.

I mostly remember having numb feet and dreaming of the car heater, but over time Grandpa Perry built a portable shack. We'd set our tip-ups outside, then return to the shack to jig for crappies and sunfish. Grandpa always brought candy bars, and he also knew how to use a can opener, so I also recall the hiss of his little gas stove bubbling a can of beans or maybe Spaghetti-Os. These are the moments when the young ones discover that fishing is only tangentially about fish.

That said, unlike Grandpa Peterson (he was a good grandpa too, his talents lay elsewhere), Grandpa Perry was a master at frying fish up in a pan, and they were usually sizzling in the kitchen by the time our toes were thawing out, so there was incentive to focus on the task at hand.

I haven't been ice fishing in years, and there is the temptation to cinch a ribbon on this piece by refreshing my resolve to do so, but the calendar isn't looking conducive. The weather, on the other hand, is turning to an extended cold stretch. The ice is gonna thicken up fast. So for all you set to set out, I wish you many a nibble and the fishiest of all hyphenated blessings: "Tip-up!"

Failing Farmhouse

Our old farmhouse continues to age out. Just this week I noticed a fresh gap between the porch and the main foundation. Either we had a small earthquake or it's just more entropy. I assume and prefer the latter. The gradual decline into disorder is a form of reverse poetics in which the carefully structured stanzas slowly slide into free verse and slant rhyme.

This artful take does not go over well at the family meeting, especially if that meeting takes place in a basement that was dug by hand prior to rural electrification and, despite twin dehumidifiers set above the wet floor on pallets, hasn't really been brought up to speed over the interim. In this year alone there have been issues with the plumbing and the well wiring and shingles and a mysterious odor that kinda smelled like cats but not quite and it's the "but not quite" that puts a pinch in your rictus. Then there are the ongoing issues of mice and ice dams and the leak in the laundry room and the bathroom door that traps unsuspecting guests, and let's just table the rest of the list on the table that sits at a slight slant because so does the floor.

With an 1880s-vintage log cabin heart enclosed by several generations worth of additions, cobble-ups, and tack-ons, the house was never going to be a candidate for remodeling. At least not on our budget. Once when I was fixing up an old truck, a local farmer suggested it would make more sense to jack up the radiator cap and drive a new truck in under it; in the case of our house, the same line of thinking applies.

All of these things could be cured with a bulldozer and a construction loan. We've been planning for that since we moved in. Then one day fourteen years had passed, and here we sit, still planning, still wearing a circle in the rug of pros and cons, including—now that one child has left the roost—whether this is really where we'll be for any given future. Our dead end road is becoming less dead. Hammer blows and nail guns echo through the wintry woods. The city is creeping closer. I don't dread it anymore. Reverse entropy, I guess. Everybody moved here sometime. We are susceptible to thinking time stops moving when we do. Here in our old farmhouse we have options. This puts us in the privileged percentile, period.

Something will need to be done. The poetics of entropy don't stack up against a cracked pipe in a sketchy crawl space. But last week when the straight-line winds roared over the hill and we took our blankets downstairs and slept against the foot-thick logs hand-squared by some long-gone settler, we sure weren't longing for drywall. Last night when we gathered on the creaking floorboards around the woodstove with family from out of town and sang Christmas carols accompanied by our daughter playing guitar, we weren't coveting a fully wired basement entertainment center. And while triple-pane windows would be sweet, this morning at dawn my view to the day was obscured by a windowpane swabbed in illuminated frost through which the sun busted into a thousand sparkles.

As obstructed views go, I'll take it.

Swingset Reset

LAST WEEK'S WINDS whipped knots into the swing set chains. I discovered this while working out at my personal health club, currently located in our granary, which overlooks the swing set, which is planted on the brow of a hill with a view to the valley below.

Based on a date scrawled in the concrete, the granary was constructed just after World War II. It is unheated and uninsulated, so there is little point in keeping the doors closed while getting fit. Unless we are under blizzard conditions, I roll them open so I can enjoy some vista with my misery.

"Getting fit" is a relative and recurrent reference dating back to my early 30s when I first noticed I could no longer train for a 5K run in under two weeks. Like many self-improving humans, I tend to go in bursts and underachieve, propelled by the belief that next week I am really gonna buckle down and get after it.

And yet, over the past year-and-a-half, I have managed to put together and keep together a fundamental program combining a treadmill desk, a smattering of hill sprints, and the lifting of heavy stuff. At one point I rewarded myself for sticking with it by purchasing a set of used weights, thus allowing me to upgrade from the steel fence post and concrete blocks I had been using. The used equipment has a little rust on it, which is about right. I also just checked the receipt and see I made the purchase on April Fool's Day. Time will tell.

The last time I tried working out in an actual gym it had mirrors everywhere, and I had to leave because I found it impossible to stop snickering at the big boys side-eying their triceps while acting like they weren't side-eying their triceps. I took my dough-ball self out of there before some striated studmuffin force-fed me a dumbbell.

And so I return to the mirrorless granary. Last thing I need is to contemplate the veins popping on my bald head as I grunt through my routine, not that I'd see them anyways as this time of year I work out in a cap, barn boots, and a chore jacket. Chugging up a snow-covered hill in rubberized footwear purchased at a farm store is my version of running wind sprints on the beach.

So there I was, deadlifting with my sweaty face to the open air, when I noticed those snarled chains. My obsessive gene wouldn't let it go, so I finished the set and went straight to the untangling. Apparently the wind had flipped the flat seats around and around, over and over, gnarling the links into the devil's own macramé. One swing had been flung around a leg of the frame then snugged into a knot that would have done a sailor proud.

Given time, persistence, and physics, nature performs marvelous tricks. An invisible wind moves an iron chain. A fool walks in place, lifts things that don't need lifting, runs uphill despite not being chased, and a year later feels fitter, if not leaner. Most of all the fool is grateful for the air, drawn one cool lungful at a time as he undoes the knots, the world for a moment still and untwisted.

Michael Perry

ORWELL

In an ongoing attempt to wrest my brain away from the hypnotic scroll and tap of contemporary dread and effervescence, this week I sat myself down and read the text of the 2021 Orwell Memorial Lecture, as delivered by the novelist Ian McEwen. It quite naturally features George Orwell, with a cameo by Albert Camus, a pop-in by Henry James, and a line of poetry from W.H. Auden.

I am tempted to preemptively self-deprecate by invoking my deer rifle and my snowplow and shucks and my enduring inability to recite the definition of words like "heuristic" and "ontological" (just this morning I had to look up the word "prosody" for the forty-third time), but in fact I like reading things written by smart people. One lives in hope that a shard of secondhand intellect might ricochet from the page, hit my thick skull with sufficient velocity to throw a spark, and therewith energize some dormant cerebral neuron. I still won't be able to fix the brakes on a 1994 Chevy Silverado.

The article in question focused on Orwell's wrestling with whether he should write about the troubles of the world or fight the troubles of the world. Ultimately he did both, writing *Animal Farm* and *1984* but also taking a bullet to the throat during the Spanish Civil War. He emerged pessimistic and disillusioned, but the latter is a form of learning. After framing Orwell's state of mind with two lines of Auden ("As the clever hopes expire/of a low dishonest decade"), McEwen surmises that *Animal Farm* is powerful because it was "liberated by its pessimism" to speak the truth about human nature.

I am neither here nor qualified to parse the work of Orwell or the other fellows named above; in reading an essay of this sort, I am simply searching for clues to guide my own comportment or at the very least how to row my boat in something other than a circle. For instance, when McEwen writes of Orwell's worrying over "the intrusion of ideology [and] 'correct' thinking into private thought and public discourse," I find myself nodding but also checking myself for signs of what Orwell called "orthodoxy sniffing." A squirmy term, as it should be.

Orwell does not let us off the hook. At his best, he is the hook. But in a diary entry written shortly after prime minister Neville Chamberlain announced that England was at war with Germany, Orwell noted the weeds were overtaking his garden, the last of his peas had kinda just petered out, and one of his pumpkins was "the size of a billiard ball." On the other hand, he noted that his turnips, carrots, and runner beans were doing well.

This leads McEwen to invoke the importance of "the poetry of the everyday," to cite the author John Updike's desire to "give the mundane its beautiful due," and finally, to quote Henry James, specifically a passage in which he exhorts the reader not to invest too heavily in optimism or pessimism, but rather to simply "catch the colour of life itself." This, in a time of trouble, is a great privilege. And if so allowed, so I shall do.

*